THE MANUFACTURER'S GUIDE TO BUSINESS MARKETING.

How Small and Midsize Companies Can Increase Profits With Limited Resources

Michael P. Collins

Published by
MPC Management

2237 NE 203rd Ave.
Fairview, Oregon
97024
(503) 661-1156

D1417366

Library of Congress Cataloging-in-Publication Data

Collins, Michael P.
   The manufacturer's guide to business marketing : how small and
midsize companies can increase profits with limited resources /
Michael P. Collins.
        p.   cm.
   Includes index.
   ISBN 1-55623-837-1
   1. Marketing–Management.   2. Small business—Management.
I. Title.
HF5415.13.C643   1995
658.8—dc20   94–11216

Printed in the United States of America
   2 3 4 5 6 7 8 9 0   1 0 9

Preface

There are plenty of books on the subject of marketing, but most of them focus on consumer marketing. This book focuses on business marketing: on the selling, advertising, distribution, and product development techniques used by companies that manufacture products for sale to other businesses.

The world of manufacturing is undergoing profound changes. A 1987 report from the US Office of Technology Assessment predicted:

> During the next two decades, new technologies, rapid increases in foreign trade, and the tastes and values of a new generation of Americans are likely to reshape virtually every product, every service, and every job in the U.S. These forces will shake the foundation of the most secure American businesses.

The manufacturing sector is already experiencing the transformation forecasted in that report. Today, producers of everything from computers to machine tools to chemicals are struggling to retain their customers in the face of sharply rising competition, much of it from overseas. With more and more choices available to them, customers are demanding—and getting—higher quality, more innovation, and better service, at lower cost. Furthermore, they are turning away from companies that don't deliver precisely what they want.

The Rise of Small and Midsize Manufacturers

This environment presents a tremendous opportunity for small to midsize manufacturers (SMMs). Many large manufacturers are cumbersome bureaucracies; they don't have the speed and flexibility needed to respond to the whirlwind changes in today's marketplace. By contrast, SMMs are lean, flexible, and innovative, and they can move quickly to satisfy customers' accelerating demands.

While small may be beautiful, size alone is no guarantee of success. Only the SMMs that learn how to become customer-driven, that allow their customers to dictate the quality and kinds of products and services to offer, will emerge as winners in the new economy.

Unfortunately, in my experience most SMMs are not customer-driven; they are sales-driven. Generating more sales is almost always their primary objective. In fact, they exhibit a general tendency to try to solve all their problems with more sales volume. In the quest for more sales, their battle cry becomes, "Any customer is a good customer."

I believe the solution to increased competition is *not* to bring in just any customer but to win the business of a select group of customers. The small manufacturers that are thriving today are the ones that are practicing *niche marketing*—focusing on a specific group of customers, learning their needs, and designing products and services to meet these needs better than their competitors do.

SMMs who thrived in the past without knowing much about their customers will soon find themselves losing their business to more aggressive (translated: more customer-driven) competitors..

American manufacturers are on a crusade to improve quality and to achieve something called *total customer satisfaction*. This can't happen unless SMMs make the transformation from sales-driven to customer-driven, market-oriented organizations. This book is dedicated to showing them how.

Goals of the Book

I have written this book with six goals in mind:

1. To show readers that "shotgun marketing"—selling anything to any customer—costs SMMs a fortune, in terms of lost revenues and opportunities, and will not allow them to achieve quality goals and total customer satisfaction.

2. To teach small manufacturers simple techniques for monitoring their customers' needs and responding quickly and effectively to their changing demands.

3. To demonstrate the benefits of niche marketing, and to show readers how to focus their limited resources on the *right* customers rather than simply going after *more* customers.

4. To show SMMs how to carry out an effective marketing strategy with limited resources. SMMs are not miniature versions of their Fortune 500 competitors. They have limited time, limited staff, and severely restricted marketing budgets. What works for Caterpillar Tractor won't work for them. In this book, I'll show how effective

business marketing strategies can be implemented on a shoestring budget.

5. To translate complex marketing ideas and concepts into practical, step-by-step solutions to the everyday problems of SMMs, written in language they can understand.

6. To show SMMs how to market high-priced, complex products with long sales cycles. Such products require specialized and often unique marketing strategies that can't be found in most marketing books, classes, and seminars.

Who Should Read This Book?

This book should be read by anyone who works for a small or midsize manufacturing company, including:

- **Founders, owners, and senior executives** of small and midsize manufacturing firms who want to develop cost-effective marketing strategies that can improve their profit picture.

- **Sales and marketing managers** who want to develop effective marketing and sales plans.

- **Salespeople** who are trained in the sales end of manufacturing and want to understand and benefit from the marketing side of the game should benefit from the ideas presented in the book.

- **Engineers, production workers, and other nonmarketing employees** will be helped to understand the importance of being customer-driven and quality-minded.

- **Industrial distributors and manufacturing representatives** will find many ideas on how to support and provide market direction to the companies who represent SMMs.

- **Large manufacturers'** salespeople, especially those who have been hired into industrial sales but have never learned the basics of industrial or business marketing. Employees of companies that are downsizing may want to explore the advantages of the SMM.

This book also is an ideal guide for **business professors and trainers.** The real-world examples and practical applications throughout the book provide an added dimension to classroom training, and will help to attract small business owners and operators who would not attend purely academic courses.

Practical, Useful Advice

This is a "how-to" book that blends formal marketing strategies with the street smarts I have acquired in the course of working for small and mid-size manufacturers over the last 30 years. The ideas presented in these pages are based on *proven marketing techniques,* on the real-life successes and failures of SMMs in a wide variety of industries. Along the way, I've included dozens of anecdotes and examples of companies that are thriving today as a result of mastering these techniques.

For many years, SMM companies have been my primary customers. In developing this book, I have taken my own advice and spent a lot of time researching my customers' needs and examining what works or doesn't work for them when it comes to marketing. As a result, I believe I've produced a product that fits the needs of small manufacturers better than any other marketing book. I hope you will agree.

Michael P. Collins

Acknowledgments

My interest in business marketing started with my first job out of college. No book I had read and no class I had attended prepared me for the realities of business marketing. I have since had the opportunity to work for and with many manufacturers, small and large. These experiences, and the lessons I learned from many small companies with limited resources have significantly influenced the ideas in this book.

I also owe a debt of gratitude to the people whom I interviewed for this book, particularly Dick Sears, Rich Rice, Kathy Wakefield, Larry Wade, Don Dauterman, and Jerry Sivin, who gave up many hours of their valuable time to help me explain their stories.

My heartfelt thanks go to my literary agent, Laurie Harper, and my editor, Jeanine Drew, who kept their heads during the difficult periods. My deepest gratitude goes to the team who reviewed the original material: Phil Dickie, Jack McNally, Larry Buzan, and Kim Millier. These people kept me focused on the great differences among industrial products and the need to match marketing strategies to product type. They also continually reminded me of the challenges of doing effective business marketing on a limited budget.

M.P.C.

Contents

Introduction

Twenty-five years ago, those of us who were beginning our careers with large US manufacturing companies felt so secure that we were almost bored with the idea of a "job for life." We just assumed that America's flagship companies would keep on growing indefinitely.

I remember, when I was just out of college and starting my first job, being escorted to a large auditorium with all the other trainees. We listened to a lecture on the benefits of staying with the corporation until retirement. I will never forget the graph we were shown; it projected lift truck sales growing without interruption from 1965 until the end of the century. Who could have anticipated that, within 15 years, foreign competition, several recessions, and a changing economy would not only eliminate the job of everyone sitting in that room but cause most of the US lift truck industry to shift to offshore manufacturing?

It took me and many other people several years to figure out that what happened in the lift truck industry was not an isolated phenomenon. By the late 1970s, it was becoming clear that every sector of the economy was drastically changing. The changes accelerated in the 1980s, as more industries fell victim to a flood of new foreign products and many blue-chip corporations were taken over by other companies or corporate raiders.

The good old days of mass production seemed to be drawing to an end. The only thing that seemed certain was that business in the United States had changed dramatically and would probably go on changing, at least through the 1990s.

One of the most profound shifts in the decade of the 1980s was the downsizing of America's largest corporations. The decline was particularly dramatic in the manufacturing sector. In 1979, the 500 largest companies in the United States employed 16.2 million workers, or 80 percent of the total manufacturing work force. By 1989, the top 500 companies employed only 12.5 million workers, or about 60 percent of the manufacturing work force.[1]

During that 10-year period, more than 3.7 million manufacturing workers from Fortune 500 companies lost their jobs.[2]

THE EMERGENCE OF SMALL MANUFACTURERS

But there is good news mixed with the bad. While the 1980s and early 1990s saw huge layoffs, this period also witnessed the unleashing of a new wave of entrepreneurship. Small business emerged as a new and powerful force in the economy. Between 1980 and 1989, 19 million new jobs were created, and the vast majority of these jobs were created by companies with fewer than 250 employees.[3]

Nowhere is this entrepreneurship phenomenon more visible than in the manufacturing sector. While many experts predicted that manufacturing would decline as the United States shifted to an information economy, others recognized that it would flourish—but only within certain segments.

In the early 1980s, Michael Piore and Charles Sable of Massachusetts Institute of Technology (MIT) in Cambridge were among the first to predict the demise of mass production and the shift toward small manufacturers with flexible manufacturing systems that can produce short production runs, customized products, and fast deliveries. Piore and Sable envisioned that new, flexible technologies, such as the microcomputer and numerically controlled machine tools, would lower the cost of customized and batch products, thus allowing companies to offer a wide variety of new products to a fast-changing market. They wrote:

> We are moving away from a situation where the small company was typically subordinated to the large company and operated largely at its direction, and we're moving toward a situation where the small company is the dynamic leading edge of the economy.[4]

Their analysis was right on target. Today the bright stars of US manufacturing are the thousands of small to midsize manufacturers (SMMs) that have always lived in the shadows of their big brothers. SMMs grew and proliferated faster in the 1980s than in any other decade of this century.

A new generation of SMMs is not only growing but flourishing in the changing economy. These are exciting times for SMMs. There will be a host of opportunities available to them in the coming decade as the economy continues to shift, but new approaches in managing and marketing will be required to take advantage of these opportunities.

The central message of this book is that the SMMs that become proficient at business marketing are going to have the best chance of surviving and thriving in the new economy. To do this, they will have to adopt three fundamental strategies: (1) they must focus on improving profit performance, not higher sales volume; (2) they must become customer-driven—a major change for most SMMs; and (3) they must target specific markets and customers, and must tailor their products and services to satisfy these markets and customers.

SMMs are already being forced by demands for higher quality to adapt new technologies, to empower work teams, and to develop new management techniques and systems. A similar educational process will be needed in the area of marketing, particularly for the thousands of small family-owned and family-managed companies that in the past depended on a few large customers to stay alive. Many of these companies do not understand some of the basics of business marketing. They are not used to developing marketing programs, surveying customers, identifying market niches, or developing effective marketing plans. This book will show them how to go about it.

Over the years I have suggested numerous classes, books, articles, and workshops to SMMs who wanted to know more about business marketing. The feedback I get is always the same. People complain that the marketing information they gain from these sources is "nice to know" but doesn't seem to translate into increased sales or profit.

My philosophy is that if you can't understand and use a marketing idea or solution in the near term, it's probably not worth reading about. And you won't find it in this book. What you *will* find are plenty of concrete, practical suggestions for solving the marketing problems you face every day.

My hope is that this book will give you some practical new insights into business marketing and inspire you to redesign your company into a customer-driven business that thrives on change.

NOTES

1. John Case, *From the Ground Up* (New York: Simon and Schuster, 1992), pp. 32–33. The case study drew heavily on the works of Zoltan J Zacs, David B Ausretsch, David L Birch, Bruce Phillips, and Catherine Armington.
2. Ibid., pp. 32–33.
3. Ibid., p. 33.
4. The Second Industrial Revolution, FACE TO FACE, INC., September 1985, p. 36.

Chapter One

Choosing the Right Path
How to Avoid the Hazards of Shotgun Marketing

"Cheshire Puss," she began,
rather timidly....

"Would you tell me, please,
which way I ought to go from here?"

"That depends a good deal on
where you want to get to,"
said the Cat.

"I don't care where, said Alice.
"Then it doesn't matter which
way you go," said the Cat.

"—so long as I get *somewhere,*"
Alice added as an explanation.

"Oh, you're sure to do that,"
said the Cat, "if you only
walk long enough."

Lewis Carroll, *Alice's Adventures in Wonderland*

This book is about choosing the right path—the right market niche, the right product, the right sales and marketing strategies, and, above all, the right customers. I believe that choosing the right customers is the most important decision a manufacturing company makes. A good choice, or a bad one, will have long-term effects on the resources, organization, management, and capital of the company. If the decision is wrong, a lot of money will be wasted on new products, services, promotion, and distribution channels designed for customers who can't or won't buy again. In the worst case, a wrong decision can lead the company into bankruptcy.

FACING THE FACTS

Much of what is written about marketing focuses on strategies used by large corporations. These companies have marketing departments, experience, large budgets, and the management depth and marketing savvy to be successful business marketers. But what about the smaller manufacturers, particularly the thousands of family businesses and privately owned companies that have very limited resources?

All small and midsize manufacturers suffer to some degree from the *FACTS*: **fear** (of making a wrong decision that will put them out of business), limited **access** to capital, **cash** flow problems, limited **time,** and limited or no **staff.** These are real day-to-day problems that must be considered in devising any marketing strategy, and the smaller the company, the worse the resource limitations.

Accepting that FACTS is the reality of most small and midsize manufacturers (SMMs), how can these companies become effective marketers? By carefully focusing their marketing strategies to get the most out of their limited resources. Unfortunately, many SMMs subscribe to certain marketing myths that can quickly exhaust their precious resources and lead them down the path of bankruptcy rather than along the road to success.

MARKETING MYTHS

There are thousands of examples of entrepreneurs who have launched small manufacturing firms that develop innovative product ideas but never seem to find the path to profitability. In my experience, most of these owners subscribe to four widely accepted myths about marketing and sales that inevitably put them on the wrong path.

Myth #1: More Sales = More Profits

A good friend of mine who was once the sales manager of a small hydraulics manufacturer described an intense meeting with the owner in which the strategic problems of the company were being discussed. Charlie was only halfway through explaining the cash flow, production, service, and indebtedness problems facing the company when the owner became red in the face, pounded his fist on the table and said, "What we need around here is more sales and less bellyaching!"

Over the years, "more sales" has become the rallying cry of most SMMs. The owners and managers of these firms believe that the growth of sales is the answer to all their problems. It is almost sacrilegious to suggest otherwise, to point out that, in fact, more sales could possibly be **bad** for the company—but it's true. Many small manufacturers achieve their sales forecasts, or even attain record sales, but never generate the profits they dream about. The reasons are simple:

- If sales costs are too high, selling more will only produce more red ink for the company.
- More sales means more accounts payable; if a company has limited financing and serious cash flow problems, sales growth can catapult it into bankruptcy.
- More sales can't solve quality or service problems, or many other problems that affect profitability. In fact, more sales may exacerbate these problems.

Obviously, sales growth is **not** synonymous with profit growth; but it is a popular marketing focus, because measuring sales is easier than managing profitability.

Myth #2: Any Customer Is a Good Customer

The second marketing myth is closely related to the first. It is a widely held belief that a small company should market to any customer who is willing to buy, regardless of selling costs or the products and services the customer requires.

It is futile to expect the SMM to adequately serve a wide variety of customers. By definition, small companies have limited resources. They do not have the time or money to be all things to all people. If they try, the end result will inevitably be poor quality, lousy service, and lost customers.

Myth #3: Build a Better Mousetrap, and the World Will Buy It

In the late 1960s, I worked for a company that decided to redesign all its product lines at one time. Company management felt that the engineering staff had the experience and wisdom to make all the design decisions, so little time was spent asking customers their opinions. The result was a disastrous product introduction that cost the company millions of dollars in warranty costs, service expenses, and lost customers, due to faulty product design. The problems took years to correct and threatened the loss of the company's most profitable markets.

I have always been amazed at how willing manufacturing companies are to spend $250,000 on research and development (R&D) and prototype development, while they will agonize over spending $2,500 on surveying their customers about what kinds of products they might want to buy.

In some cases, SMMs do manage to develop products that are highly marketable, even without consulting prospective customers. However, because most of them have no systematic way of targeting the customers who might be interested (see Myth #2), their products languish on warehouse shelves.

Myth #4: Macro Markets Are More Profitable than Niche Markets

In my experience, SMMs waste vast amounts of time and money trying to compete in large markets when they should be focusing on a market niche they truly can support. Too many small companies believe there are safety and riches in macro markets. They believe they can sneak into a large market and skim off a tiny share of a huge pie that nobody will miss.

This myth can be discerned in the business plan of virtually every start-up company. Here's a typical expression of the myth: "The 1992 sales of single-board computers in the United States exceeded $1 billion. Annual sales of Acme's industrial computers equivalent to 1 percent of this market would translate into approximately 10,000 units, or $100 million in gross sales."

This statement is totally erroneous. It is naive to expect that just because a market is huge, a small company can siphon off a piece of it—even 1 percent of it—without a carefully focused marketing effort. The fact is, the bigger the market, the more attractive it is to large companies with large marketing budgets.

The small firm can't realistically expect to be able to compete against the resources of the giants. The only real safety for an SMM is to focus on a small niche the company can defend, one that is too small to interest the larger companies.

THE PERILS OF SHOTGUN MARKETING

Taken together, these four myths describe the philosophy of **shotgun marketing.** Shotgun marketing is not targeted at the customers who need the product; it is aimed at broad groups of buyers, in the hopes of hitting the few who do have a need. Shotgun marketing is like firing a shotgun into the forest in the hope that you will kill something for dinner. It is very expensive (takes a lot of shots), and you may not like the results (wounded grizzly bears, or unhappy customers).

Shotgun marketing is a poor use of limited marketing dollars. It is extremely difficult for a company to design new products, advertise, provide appropriate customer services, or efficiently cover a sales territory if it can't identify specific customers and uncover their needs.

It is also difficult to provide high-quality products and services when a company practices shotgunning, because **all the company's resources are devoted to finding more customers.** There is little time or money left to focus on satisfying current customers—including the most profitable customers. (Ironically, there always seems to be enough time and money to fix the problems caused by unprofitable customers.)

Low Repeat Business

Selling to any and every customer is a costly proposition, but losing a repeat customer is an even more expensive problem associated with shotgun marketing. Because of the inevitable quality and service problems that come with shotgunning, companies that practice it cannot hope to retain a high percentage of their customers or to maintain a high level of profitability.

Figure 1–1 shows why customers become more profitable over time. In the beginning (in the first year), a typical new customer costs the company money (advertising and selling costs) to acquire. In the second year, the company begins to make a profit. Satisfied customers purchase more in the second year than in the first year, which increases profits sharply. Longer-term customers have learned how to buy more efficiently. Less time (and less money) is spent in educating them about product specifications, how to read drawings, and so forth. Reduced operating costs translate into greater profits. Satisfied long-term customers generate even more profit by referring new customers to the company. The final profit component is that the company gains profit from being able to charge a premium price.[1]

FIGURE 1–1
Retaining Customers Increases Profit

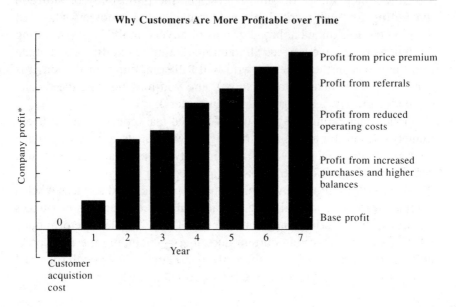

Why Customers Are More Profitable over Time

*This pattern is based on our experience in many industries.

Source: Reprinted by permission of *Harvard Business Review.* An exhibit from "Zero Defections: Quality Comes to Services" by Frederick F Reichheld and W Earl Sasser, Jr., September–October 1990. Copyright © 1990 by the President and Fellows of Harvard College; all rights reserved.

The Case of Hi-Tech Corporation

A few of the numerous problems associated with shotgun marketing are illustrated in the following case study. The case is based on the true story of a firm I'll call Hi-Tech Corporation, whose commitment to shotgun marketing ultimately led it to the edge of bankruptcy.

Hi-Tech was founded by three entrepreneurial engineers in 1983, when the use of business computers was exploding with new applications. The company manufactured single-board computers for industrial applications.

Like most start-up companies with little cash, Hi-Tech got off the ground with a shotgun mail-order program that reached everyone from hobbyists working in their basements to Fortune 500 company engineers designing plant production systems. Using this technique, Hi-Tech built up sales volume to a point at which it was acquiring more than 250 new customers every year. This is where the trouble began.

As sales grew, Hi-Tech began experiencing a variety of technical, quality, and service problems. Many customers were interested enough to experiment with Hi-Tech's products, but each customer group wanted a product that fit its own very specific application. This meant Hi-Tech was handling widely varying applications, from nuclear power plants to robot controls, each requiring a great deal of technical support. In trying to serve a wide variety of customer groups, Hi-Tech wasn't supporting any of them well. As a result, repeat customers accounted for less than 15 percent of the company's annual revenues.

Hi-Tech spent a lot of money on advertising to find new customers, but it didn't make money on the new accounts, because they were too costly to acquire. The company had an ongoing product development program, but many new products never found many interested buyers, since all new products were invented by the owners with no customer input.

The owners recognized these problems, but they believed that most of them would be solved by additional sales volume. In part, they were right; a 25 percent annual growth rate between 1985 and 1989 provided the funds to continue expanding operations.

By 1989, the company had surpassed $1 million in sales, and some major original equipment manufacturers (OEMs) were beginning to use the company's single-board computers as primary controls in their own products. This growth accelerated the company's problems to the point where the owners became extremely defensive and began avoiding customers altogether. When the 1990 recession came, Hi-Tech simply didn't have the customer base or the profitability to sustain itself.

The company subsequently lost most of its OEM customers and drifted into a state of perpetual cash flow problems. Hi-Tech is now essentially back to where it started—desperately hunting for new customers to keep the doors open.

The tragedy of this story is that the owners of Hi-Tech could easily have avoided their serious financial problems. They were given many opportunities to focus on specific customer groups and win their loyalty, rather than going after any and all customers. Some customers went out of their way to explain their needs and even to suggest quality, support, and service programs. The owners had several chances to turn their situation around, but they couldn't quite see their opportunities through the smoke of their shotgun blasts.

How Can Something So Bad Be So Popular?

Shotgun marketing is very expensive and almost always results in erratic profitability and dissatisfied customers. It can create more quality and customer service problems than the company can ever hope to handle. There are major headaches involved in shotgun marketing that can make a firm's day-to-day working atmosphere miserable, leading to high employee turnover.

Why is this ineffective strategy so popular with small manufacturers? The answer is simple: **shotgunning is the easiest approach to marketing.** It requires little thought and no planning. A company doesn't have to understand its markets, profile its customers, know its product costs, or even deal with its customers' needs (until after the sale, when the customers begin reporting problems).

Shotgunning appeals to the entrepreneurial spirit; it allows the owners of a company to run it by the seat of their pants. It is particularly appealing to entrepreneurs who love products and technology but are uncomfortable with customers or the "people" side of the business. It is action-oriented, guaranteed to produce crisis and drama. Shotgun marketing can take the company on a wild, exciting ride, but most people burn out on the problems it causes.

Exercise: Is Your Company a Shotgun Marketer?

How can you determine whether your company is going down the perilous path of shotgun marketing? The checklist in Figure 1–2 will help. The figure shows 23 typical symptoms of shotgun marketing. Each of these symptoms is based on the real-life problems of small and midsize manufacturers I have worked with over the years. Go down the list, point by point, and check each comment that generally fits the description of how your company operates.

Now rate yourself, assigning 5 points to each checkmark, and total your score. If your score is 25 or less, you are probably a successful and profitable niche marketer who is doing many things right. This book will confirm and explain some things you are intuitively doing right and provide some tips on how to design an even better marketing plan, with many examples of how other companies have done it.

If your score is greater than 25, you had better take a hard look at your marketing program and the ways you are trying to satisfy customers. You

FIGURE 1–2
The Shotgun Checklist

	Yes	No
Distribution		
1. Agents and/or distributors complain that your company doesn't provide good market direction or support.	___	___
2. Agents and/or distributors are devoting more time to other manufacturers' products than to yours.	___	___
3. Selling costs of your current sales and distribution are too high to cover small or low-volume accounts.	___	___
4. Agents and distributors complain that sales coverage is not defined, and they are unfairly judged by the factory.	___	___
Sales		
5. Some very large customers make demands that are beyond the ability of the individual salesperson.	___	___
6. Some of your customers are credit problems because no one checked them out during the rush to get the order.	___	___
7. Salespeople sell to any customer, regardless of size, selling costs, or geographic location.	___	___
8. Salespeople qualify most of their prospects face-to-face rather than by phoning every lead in advance.	___	___
9. Repeat sales from existing customers are low.	___	___
10. Salespeople haven't identified the most valuable customers (MVCs) who have the best future profit potential.	___	___
11. The company has a tendency to solve most production, cash flow, and other problems by seeking more sales.	___	___
12. Salespeople don't know the cost of a sales call.	___	___
Product		
13. New products don't sell well after their introduction and must be modified before they can generate sales.	___	___
14. Products are not developed with specific end-user benefits in mind.	___	___
15. Customers complain that your products and services don't fit their specific needs.	___	___
16. Decisions about products and services are made without asking customers for their input.	___	___
Advertising		
17. Few advertising inquiries are called and qualified.	___	___
18. Few or no sales are traced back to advertising.	___	___

FIGURE 1–2 *(concluded)*

	Yes	No
19. Product advertisements and messages are not directed at any specific market niche or group of customers.	___	___
Customer Satisfaction		
20. The company does not conduct customer surveys or have ways to monitor changing needs.	___	___
21. Customers complain that the quality of your services and technical support does not meet their expectations.	___	___
22. Customers file warranty claims and complain about the quality of your products.	___	___
23. No one tracks lost orders to find out why customers decided to buy competitor's products.	___	___

have far too many shotgun symptoms, and there's a good chance that you are not generating nearly the amount of profit you deserve.

Turning Problems into Opportunities

You have now developed a list of some of the most important problems facing your company. The good news is that it's relatively easy to isolate and measure the problems. With a bit of determination, your company's problems can be corrected and turned into profit opportunities. That is the subject of the rest of this book.

Throughout the book, I'll provide solutions to all the shotgun marketing problems highlighted in the checklist in Figure 1–2. I'll include numerous examples of companies who have boosted their bottom lines, increased customer retention, and satisfied their customers' needs by eliminating shotgun symptoms and developing more effective, niche marketing strategies.

* * * * *

The first step on your path to business marketing success is to learn all you can about your customers—the focus of Chapter 2.

KEY POINT

Deciding to choose the right customers is one of the most important decisions a small manufacturing company can make. Shotgun marketing is an inefficient, high-cost marketing approach which usually results in low profitability and a high number of quality, service, and customer problems.

SUGGESTED ACTION

Select three or four problems from the checklist in Figure 1–2. Form a team to analyze the costs of the problems and their impact on customers, and to devise strategies for solving them.

NOTES

1. Frederick F Reichheld and W Earl Sasser, Jr., "Zero Defections: Quality Comes to Services," *Harvard Business Review,* September–October 1990, p. 108.

Chapter Two

Determining Customers' Wants and Needs

The first essential task in business marketing, is to develop a profile of your customers—find out who they are, and which are the most valuable; define their wants and needs; understand why they buy from your company, and why from competitors; and develop a system for gathering information from them on a regular basis.

Business customers want high-quality, high-value products and services that meet their needs, with the emphasis on *their* needs, not yours. The way to find out those needs is to profile customers on a regular basis.

For many reasons, including the ones listed below, it is important for you to spend time gathering information about your customers and learning about their needs.

1. Finding out in detail what customers want and need virtually always results in new sales opportunities.

2. Developing a profile of your best customers is the quickest and easiest way to find more customers like them.

3. Understanding your customers' needs will help you retain a higher percentage of existing customers and will enable you to sell more to them, more profitably.

4. Knowing your customers' needs is absolutely necessary if you plan to implement a quality program, because quality must be defined on the customer's terms, not yours.

5. Customers appreciate suppliers who are interested enough to inquire about their problems and to attempt to better meet their needs. Customers' appreciation translates into increased sales.

6. For all the reasons listed above, profiling your customers will give you a significant advantage over your competitors.

Unfortunately, while owners and managers of small and midsize manufacturers (SMMs) can tell you almost anything about their production processes, technologies, and products, most have little in-depth information about their customers. This is partly because of their strong product orientation. A more important reason is that most small companies simply don't know how to systematically gather customer information. This chapter will outline exactly how to go about it.

BUILDING A CUSTOMER DATABASE

Building a customer database is the first step in developing a complete customer profile. The time and money spent in developing such a database will be repaid many times over in the form of additional sales and competitive advantage. (See Figure 2–1.)

The process of developing a customer database begins with an examination of customer records to find out precisely who is buying from the company. Most SMMs keep basic customer lists and routinely collect an enormous amount of customer data. These customer records are a gold mine of useful marketing information, but, in my experience, few SMMs keep their records in a form that is useful for marketing purposes. In most cases, these records are not viewed as important. As a result, they aren't maintained or updated, or their upkeep is given a low priority.

Often, even when a company has computerized its customer records, the information can't be easily accessed or manipulated—that is, broken out by product line or volume of sales of a particular customer during a certain time period. Getting the desired historical data may involve weeks of computer programming. In one instance in response to my request for information, a client printed out a 500-page document showing every customer the company had sold to since 1970. Unfortunately, this was of little use since more than two-thirds of the accounts were no longer active, or the address information was out of date.

The following four items are essential components of every customer database. (Refer to the circled numbers in Figure 2–1.) These pieces of information will allow you to identify potential markets and customers, to generate targeted mailings, and to monitor sales performance.

FIGURE 2–1
Basic Customer Database

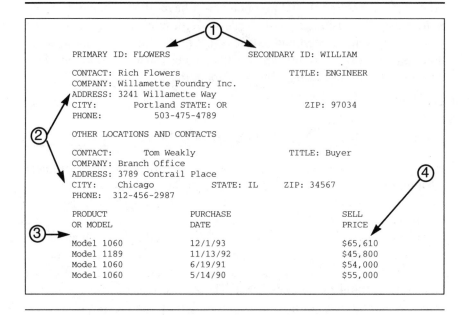

1. *Customer identification.* Most databases require an identification number or name to make it easy to find a particular customer. Often the primary identification is the contact name and the secondary identification is the name of the company.

2. *Location.* Addresses of headquarters and of all decision makers and purchasing offices should be included in the database.

3. *Product or models purchased.* This information will help you identify buying patterns by customer and market.

4. *Sales information.* Total revenue, and revenue by customer and product type. This information will enable you to spot buying trends and to determine if sales of a certain product or to a particular customer are declining or growing.

A wealth of information can be added to the customer database to make it a powerful marketing tool. (See Figure 2–2.) If you can learn to gather and utilize the following data about your customers, you will be well on your way to becoming a business marketing whiz. (Refer to the circled numbers in Figure 2–2.)

FIGURE 2–2
Comprehensive Business Marketing Database

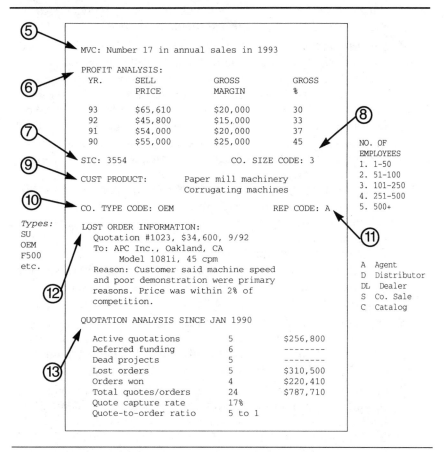

5. *Most valuable customers (MVCs).* Research has repeatedly shown that 20 percent of a company's customers generally account for 80 percent of sales; these are your most valuable customers. Once you understand the profile of your MVCs, you can develop a list of prospects who have similar characteristics and pursue their business. We'll discuss how to develop a profile of your MVCs later in this chapter.

6. *Profit analysis.* Most small manufacturers have good sales records but rarely keep detailed profit information (e.g., gross margins by product line). To become an effective business marketer, it's crucial

that you keep detailed, annual profit information by customer account, product line, and even product model. Among other things, this information will help you to identify "product dogs" that are no longer profitable and should be dropped.

7. *Standard industrial classification (SIC) codes.* These codes, published by the federal government, classify all companies by industry. You can find SIC codes for many customers in your state's manufacturing directory or in the Dun & Bradstreet *Million Dollar Directory;* both books can be found at your local library. For customers not listed in these directories, find out what products they make (if you don't already know) and look up their codes in the *Standard Industrial Classification Manual,* which is available in all major libraries.

   You can also buy lists of companies by SIC code from list brokers and from trade journal publishers. (Beware: the accuracy of the data provided by these companies varies widely. I recommend using American Business Lists, which has an excellent reputation for the quality of its manufacturing lists.)

   SIC codes can be used to generate targeted mailing lists. They can also be used to identify customer groups, or market niches; I'll discuss niche marketing in detail in Chapter 5.

8. *Company size code.* The size of the customer company, in terms of employees and revenues, is important information, since companies of different sizes require different sales and marketing strategies.

9. *Customers' products and services.* Including a list of products or services that your customers offer will enable you to identify potential new customers. For example, if you find that your model B widgets are being purchased only by small appliance manufacturers, you can target your marketing efforts to this category of potential customers.

10. *Company type code.* To simplify data input, develop a set of codes to describe the various types of customers—for example, OEM (original equipment manufacturer), F500 (Fortune 500 company), GOV (government agency), and SU (small user), etc. A given company may need two or more codes. Your goal is to be able to isolate companies of a certain type so that you can develop more effective, targeted market strategies.

11. *Rep code.* Assign a code to each sales rep, distributor, or factory salesperson. This information will be used in your sales and profit analyses (discussed in detail in Chapter 9).

12. *Lost order information.* In my experience, few small manufacturers have in place a good method of documenting lost orders or tracking which competitors won the orders they lost. This information is vital in order to ensure that future orders are won. (Later in this chapter I'll show you how to go about gathering this information.)

13. *Quotation analysis.* Many business marketers also keep a running analysis of quotations and orders. This analysis usually includes the number of orders lost and won, the dollar amount of quotations, a quotation capture rate, and the quote-to-order ratio. This gives the sales manager a very quick look at the sales history of a given account.

Getting Started

Here are some tips for getting your customer database project launched:

1. Assign one person the responsibility of maintaining the customer database, and have that person become the central point of collection for all marketing and sales information.

2. Start out with a basic database that the responsible person can easily understand and change. (Don't let programmers, accountants, or engineers get involved, or the project will turn into a programming extravaganza, resulting in a database that can't be easily accessed or updated.)

3. Ensure that maintenance of the database is as important as processing orders. Make it clear that it's a top priority for the company, and hold the designated employee accountable for maintaining it.

4. If there are information gaps, assign someone the job of calling each customer for the missing information.

IDENTIFYING MVCS

I have already noted that the top 20 percent of customers—the MVCs—generally account for 80 percent of sales. It is absolutely essential to identify your MVCs and understand what they need in great detail, for several reasons: they offer the most potential for short-term sales; they are probably the best profit producers; and their profiles will help the sales department find more companies just like them. MVCs are so valuable that you should develop specific marketing strategies to keep them.

An example will show you how to identify your MVCs. The company, which I'll call Acme Machinery, has a database of 1,000 customers, categorized by annual sales volume. The top 20 percent of Acme's customers (32 in all) accounted for 78 percent of the company's sales in 1990. By using SIC codes and determining the type of products they purchased, Acme found it easy to group the MVCs into three general categories: OEM sales (78 percent), government sales (10 percent), and small-user sales (8 percent).

Even though the OEM group accounted for approximately 80 percent of sales in all three years, Acme had devoted most of its advertising budget and other resources to finding more small commercial accounts. This resulted in a low retention rate of OEM customers, because little time or effort was spent on addressing their needs. By 1990, only 200 of the original 1,000 customers were still doing business with the company. When Acme's managers discovered this, they decided that they had to focus on developing a new sales department and the services to support OEM customers.

Who Are YOUR MVCs?

If you don't know who your MVCs are, now is the time to find out. Develop a list of your MVCs, based on sales revenues or profits; then group them into broad categories. This information is fundamental to business marketing and essential to development of effective niche marketing and sales strategy, as discussed in Chapters 5 and 9.

LOST ORDER ANALYSIS

Following up on lost orders is another way of learning about customer wants and needs. Lost order analysis is a systematic method of finding out why customers did not buy. Finding out why current or potential customers fail to give you a particular order is critical. Without this information, you wouldn't know how to prevent future lost orders, and you would have trouble retaining good customers.

It is important to find out whether you lost the order because of a product or service deficiency. When you lose an order, it's usually because a competitor offers a product or service that is perceived to be a better solution. If you don't have this information, you won't be able to modify the product, design new products, or change your strategy to offset the competitor's advantage. Lost order analysis can also give you specific information on pricing, service problems, competitor strategies, and even market trends.

Despite its importance, lost order analysis is a customer tool that is seldom used, particularly by companies that rely on shotgun marketing. For one thing, there is always strong resistance from salespeople (particularly commissioned reps), who fear that lost orders will be seen as failures and that lost order analysis will be used against them. For another, companies that practice shotgun marketing never have time to stop and find out why they lost an order; they are too busy finding the next order.

Here are some tips on how to get into the habit of tracking lost orders:

1. Explain the importance of lost order analysis to all salespeople, in terms of developing marketing strategies, designing new products, and retaining good customers.

2. Make tracking lost orders a key objective, as important as developing sales forecasts or meeting the payroll.

3. If you use manufacturing reps or distributors, include lost order analysis as part of their contracts. Make it clear that they will not be penalized for providing the information, and that you will use it to help them perform more effectively.

4. Don't accept price as an ongoing reason for lost orders from sales reps. Make an occasional follow-up call to the customer, to check on whether the reason a rep gave for a lost order is valid.

5. Follow up as soon as possible after an order has been lost, so that the circumstances will still be fresh in the customer's mind.

6. Find out who the decision maker was, and make sure to talk to that person. If necessary, find ways to get around the gatekeepers. (Treating secretaries and receptionists with courtesy will be helpful in accomplishing this end.)

7. Make your follow-up call positive; don't be a sore loser.

8. Explain to the decision maker that you want the opportunity to bid again, and you need the lost order information so that you can improve on your past performance.

9. If there is a product, quality, or service problem, explain that solving the problem is extremely important to your company, and try to get an in-depth interview.

10. For more detailed technical information, ask whether you can
    send the customer a simple follow-up questionnaire.

11. End the conversation by thanking the decision maker for the inter-
    view. Be sure to say that you intend to correct any deficiencies
    and to work harder for the customer's business in the future.

12. Follow up with a written thank-you note explaining how you are
    using the information (this keeps the door open for future sales).

IDENTIFYING CUSTOMERS' WANTS AND NEEDS

Now that you have developed at least a basic customer database, the next
task is to find out what your customers want and need. There is a big difference between wants and needs. Customers may *want* to pay a low
price for a machine for a production line, but they may *need* a heavy-duty
machine that is expensive but will last for 20 years.

Helping the customer to separate wants from needs is one of the most
critical and difficult steps in the business marketing process. It requires
empathy, the ability to stand in your customers' shoes and pay close attention to what they are saying about their problems.

There are many examples of small and large companies that either ignore or don't really understand their customers' wants and needs. They
don't seem to connect their product and service deficiencies with lost orders, or to recognize the problems they cause customers. They are not
able to stand in the customers' shoes.

Owners and senior managers of SMMs are usually well insulated from
their customers. Many of them never bother to put themselves in the customers' shoes. They don't have a formal system for gathering customer
information on a regular basis. Instead, they depend on their sales and service departments do this job adequately.

This approach is inadequate. Unless a company has a systematic way
of monitoring customers' wants and needs on a continuous basis, it can
never be sure that customers are truly satisfied.

The Acid Test

Customers' perceptions of your product quality, service, and so forth
may be far different from your own. This may explain why so many companies with good intentions and big investments in the latest quality pro-

grams still lose customers. They don't realize that the customer has a poor perception of their products and/or services until they lose the order or the account.

Here is a quick exercise to help you determine if you are in tune with your customers' wants and needs, and if you are delivering products and services that meet them: Select a customer whose orders have been declining in recent years, or a customer who has great potential but is not yet buying a large volume of a specific product. How would the customer rate your company, on a scale of 1 to 5 (with 5 being the most favorable rating), in terms of the 10 services listed in Figure 2–3? Write down the ratings you feel the customer would give your company in each of the 10 categories.

Next, ask the customer to assess your company on the same 10 factors, and compare the customer's rating with your predicted rating. Repeat this exercise with several important customers.

This exercise is designed to help you recognize that customers may perceive your products and services far differently from your expectations. This is a first step toward improving your products and services and thereby increasing your sales. You may want to change the factors listed in Figure 2–3 to fit your company and products; this form is designed to get you started.

John, the owner of a small metal fabrication company, tried the acid test on one of his customers, a large investment casting company. He was surprised to find out that the customer gave him a lower rating than he predicted in the areas of quality, price, technical support, postsale service, and the expertise of salespeople. In a meeting with the customer, John learned a great deal:

Perceived quality. The customer's quality standards were much higher than John had thought, and the customer was beginning to use them to judge suppliers, even though no written standards had been issued to suppliers.

Price. Because John's company had been awarded a few bids, he assumed his price was competitive. Discussion revealed, however, that the customer perceived John's price to be average in terms of value received. The customer knew better value for the money was available from other suppliers.

Technical support. The customer was a large company with a corporate engineering department that was biased against small companies without professional engineers and computer-aided design (CAD) tools.

FIGURE 2–3
The Acid Test

Select a customer and a product or product line. How do YOU think these customers would rate your company in the following 10 service areas? Make quick judgments on a scale of 1 to 5.

	Poor		Average		Excellent
	1	2	3	4	5
1. Delivery	____	____	____	____	____
2. Quality	____	____	____	____	____
3. Dependability	____	____	____	____	____
4. Price	____	____	____	____	____
5. Performance	____	____	____	____	____
6. Service parts	____	____	____	____	____
7. Technical support	____	____	____	____	____
8. Field service	____	____	____	____	____
9. Maintenance	____	____	____	____	____
10. Response time	____	____	____	____	____

Now ask the customer to assess the same 10 factors.

	Poor		Average		Excellent
	1	2	3	4	5
1. Delivery	____	____	____	____	____
2. Quality	____	____	____	____	____
3. Dependability	____	____	____	____	____
4. Price	____	____	____	____	____
5. Performance	____	____	____	____	____
6. Service parts	____	____	____	____	____
7. Technical support	____	____	____	____	____
8. Field service	____	____	____	____	____
9. Maintenance	____	____	____	____	____
10. Response time	____	____	____	____	____

What factors indicate strengths or weaknesses?

1. _____
2. _____
3. _____

Postsale service. The customer had an elaborate paperwork system that required, among other things, formal written procedures for returned goods. The company also demanded instant callbacks on service problems. John's company was unprepared to meet this level of service.

Sales expertise. The results of the acid test convinced John that he didn't have the salespeople or the know-how to deal with a large bureaucracy. His employees were intimidated by large, formal presentations and interdepartmental politics.

This small metal fabrication company didn't have a clue as to its big customers' wants and needs until it took the acid test. Afterward, the owner realized he would have to literally remake the company to satisfy the needs of its large customers, and decided to examine all his customers' needs more carefully.

GATHERING CUSTOMER INFORMATION

There are many ways of gathering customer information, ranging from an informal chat on the telephone, to the acid test described above, to sophisticated surveys conducted by professional research firms. Here are 11 simple data-gathering techniques:

1. *Inform your staff.* All employees who talk to customers on a regular basis should be told why customer information is important and what specific information you wish them to collect. The interviewing techniques described in Chapter 3 will help employees to gather the information.

2. *Use the sales staff.* Salespeople are excellent sources of information about customers, but they won't know how to gather information unless you tell them what you want. Use interoffice memos or sales meetings to tell your reps what you want to know about customers and their needs. It is also helpful to train them in interviewing techniques (explained in detail in Chapter 3).

3. *Review warranty forms.* Offer customers an incentive to fill out questionnaires, such as an extended warranty on a product. For example, I recently responded to a special mailer that offered the newest version of MicroSoft DOS at a 50 percent savings. I had to fill out a lengthy customer questionnaire in order to take advantage of the offer, but it was worth it to me. I'm sure the customer information was worth it to MicroSoft.

4. *Ask service people.* Technical service people have the best chance to get close to the customer. They can find out valuable information you won't likely get in a survey. Technical employees often write in a stream-of-consciousness style that leaves out beginnings, conclusions, and pertinent facts. With a little training and a list of questions, however, they can become terrific customer information providers.

5. *Follow up on shipments.* If you don't have too many customers, calling them to ask for a review of your performance after delivery is an excellent way to retain customers and improve your performance. A client who owns a software company uses this procedure with every client. His company has grown faster than he can hire software engineers.

6. *Offer training and seminars.* Many small manufacturers have discovered that offering customer training schools or field application seminars for dealers and end users produces valuable information. If you offer such programs, you will have a captive audience of customers, giving you the chance to discuss their needs with them, and to uncover new sales opportunities.

7. *Conduct focus groups.* Though use of focus groups to find out customer opinions may be too expensive for small manufacturing companies, it can pay off handsomely—particularly when they are used as a means of determining which new products or services to develop.

8. *Get designers into the field.* If you have highly engineered products, it is essential to get your product designers out to the customer's plant (especially before new products are designed, a topic that I'll discuss more in Chapter 6). Engineers take great pride in their designs and often have trouble accepting responsibility when design problems show up after the sale. The best way to break through their denial is to have them visit the customer's plant, stand right next to the malfunctioning product, and literally see the problem.

   I know this approach works because I've tried it, with good results. As a division manager of a large manufacturing company, I made a rule that all design engineers had to go out on service calls or installations at least five days per year. This small investment caused the design engineers to develop more understanding of customer needs and more empathy for customer problems. This approach led to development of more successful new products than any other technique I have ever tried.

9. *Keep customers informed.* It's a good idea to mail customers newsletters, technical briefs, product bulletins, or other information about products and product updates on a regular basis. This keeps you in communication with customers, keeps them informed, and elicits their calls.

10. *Support dealer councils.* Many SMMs which use dealers, distributors, or reps conduct regular council meetings, at which a variety of customer issues are discussed.

11. *Do regular customer surveys.* A simple performance questionnaire and some more sophisticated customer survey techniques are described below.

A Simple Performance Questionnaire

If you have never conducted a customer survey before, begin with a simple version that you can mail to all your customers periodically, to get a quick assessment of your performance. (See Figure 2–4.) A simple postcard with a return permit makes it easy for customers to respond. You can use this brief format to elicit customer input about service, product acceptance, product applications, purchasing plans, product redesign, or the performance of your salespeople or manufacturer's reps.

This simple tool can be used to generate quick feedback, particularly if the customer has had a problem with your product. It's a good idea to routinely send a postcard questionnaire a month after the products shipped. A quick response can help you nip a problem in the bud. It also presents a perfect opportunity to follow up with an in-depth conversation that could lead to additional sales. If your company needs more information than a postcard will hold, other tools, such as a fax survey, can be used.

Industrial Gasket: The Fax Survey

Industrial Gasket, Inc. (IGI), of Wilsonville, Oregon, is a small, family-owned manufacturer with 3,000 customers, and branches in five states. In 1991, the company's primary goal was to improve customer service. To achieve this goal, the company decided to find out what customers thought about its products and services, and whether IGI was accurately reading customers' wants and needs.

On the advice of the local MCI rep, IGI decided that faxing surveys to customers would be the quickest and most efficient method to gather the

FIGURE 2–4
Simple Performance Questionnaire

	Yes	*No*
1. Does the product perform to your specifications?	____	____
2. Was delivery on time and satisfactory?	____	____
3. Do we return our calls promptly?	____	____
4. Are our parts and service priced competitively?	____	____
5. Have we responded adequately with overnight repair parts, and to downtime service needs?	____	____
6. Are the operation manuals clear enough to maintain and troubleshoot our product?	____	____
7. Would you recommend our product to another company?	____	____

COMMENTS: _____

_____

_____

_____

---

information. The company looked up every customer's fax number and bought an 800 line to make it easier for customers to respond. The local phone company faxed the questionnaires overnight to all 3,000 customers. The fax survey used is shown in Figure 2–5.

The response was so good that IGI's 800 number was completely busy for the first three days. Over the next three weeks, the company continued to gather vital customer information. It found that, despite management goals, the company wasn't focused totally on its customers.

The survey revealed that the company's perception of customer needs was different from the customers' perception. Specifically:

1. IGI's quality wasn't perceived as being as high as customers' standards.

2. Customers felt that the product knowledge of inside customer service employees did not meet their expectations.

3. Outside salespeople were seen as inefficient and did not seem to have a good understanding of customer needs.

4. Response time was perceived as too slow.

5. Customers didn't want IGI's salespeople to make face-to-face calls until there was an established need.

FIGURE 2–5
Sample Fax Survey

To Our Valued Customer:

Thank you for choosing **Industrial Gasket, Inc. (IGI)** as your sealing supplier. I hope we have demonstrated a professional attitude in every aspect of our business relationship.

As we strive to provide exceptional customer service for you, we ask one small favor. Would you please fill out this short questionnaire, and **fax** it back to me today. Please use our **toll-free fax number (800 685-9043).**

I will personally review your survey. Then, using your input and suggestions, I can evaluate our service, from our customer's point of view. Be assured that this information will be for **IGI** corporate marketing use only and will serve as a guide for **IGI** as we continue our growth in the area of customer service.

Your response is greatly appreciated.

Any suggestions or comments you may have would be greatly appreciated.

1. Your application of our products is:

___ OEM ___ Maintenance ___ High-tech ___ Resale ___ Other (_____)

2. How did you first hear about **INDUSTRIAL GASKET, INC.?**

___ Yellow pages   ___ Advertising   ___ Referral

___ Salesperson   ___ Other (_____)

3. How often are you in contact with an **IGI** salesperson?

___ Daily ___ Weekly ___ Monthly ___ Other (_____)

4. On a scale of 1–4 please indicate:

How important is each of the areas to your company?

    #1 = Not important
    #2 = Somewhat important
    #3 = Relatively important
    #4 = Very important   *Circle Your Response*

A.	Quality of product material	1	2	3	4
B.	Accurate specifications of product	1	2	3	4
C.	Delivery of product when promised	1	2	3	4
D.	Salesperson knowledge of products	1	2	3	4
E.	Salesperson knowledge of YOUR needs	1	2	3	4
F.	Salesperson contact on a weekly basis	1	2	3	4
G.	Delivery of products by an IGI salesperson	1	2	3	4
H.	Convenient will-call order pickup area	1	2	3	4

As a result of the survey, IGI reorganized its entire inside and outside sales operation and got all employees to focus on customer services. Marketing manager Jason Lee commented:

> Overall, this survey has shown us that we are not an excellent service company. However, the survey has pointed out some areas which we can work on, and this information can be used to direct our efforts in our drive toward legendary customer service.[1]

Granite Rock Company: The Art of the Customer Profile

An excellent example of a small manufacturing firm that has mastered the art of profiling customers is the Granite Rock Company of Watsonville, California. Granite Rock is a 100-year-old family-owned company with operations in a dozen locations between San Francisco and Monterey, California. With $90 million in revenues in 1990, Granite Rock is one of the smaller players in the construction materials industry. Even though the company is small and the industry competes largely on the basis of price, Granite Rock is able to charge a premium for its products, because it delivers high value by listening to what its customers want.

To retain its customers year after year, Granite Rock must work hard to prove to them that its products and services are worth the extra cost. To accomplish this goal, the company devised a means of monitoring customers' changing needs and making sure that these needs are translated into products and services.

To identify customers' needs, every three or four years Granite Rock conducts detailed surveys of all its customers. Among other questions, Granite asks customers to provide their own definitions of quality and service, and to rank their most important factors in choosing a supplier.

The company also asks customers to compare its performance relative to competitors—valuable information that few manufacturing firms bother to acquire. Every year, Granite Rock conducts an opinion survey (see Figure 2–6) that amounts to a report card on the company. Each customer grades its top three suppliers (including Granite Rock) on seven measures of product quality and ten measures of customer service.

The company communicates the combined results of the surveys to all employees. The results are plotted on graphs and posted on a bulletin board at each division to show workers how they measure up against the competition.

Is all the time and effort spent on the customer surveys worth it? Dave Franceschi, of Granite Rock's quality planning department, thinks so.

FIGURE 2–6

Customer Opinion Survey: Ready Mix Concrete

THE ANNUAL REPORT CARD
Once a year, each of Granite
Rock's 12 plants sends out forms
like this one to all its customers.
The specific questions vary
slightly from plant to plant, each
of which is responsible for a
different product, but the format is
the same. Some divisions use
color-coded survey forms to
distinguish between types of
contractors. (Blue forms go to
landscapers. Masons receive
orange forms.) All the completed
forms are addressed to the
divisional headquarters, where the
results are compiled and forwarded
to the rest of the division.

THE GRADING SYSTEM
The form asks the customer to
grade its top three suppliers—one
of which is presumably Granite
Rock—on their performance in
terms of product quality and
customer service. Although there
are six grades in the scale, the
company bases its charts on the
total number of A's and B's a
supplier gets in a given category.
"A C is neutral," says Wes Clark.
"If they give you a C, they feel
there's no difference between
you and everybody else.
If they give you a D or an F,
they are just punishing you."
But A's and B's amount to
fairly uniform positive votes,
he reasons. An A is for a
job well done. A B is a
similar response from
a tougher grader.

Ready Mix Concrete
OPINION SURVEY

Please write the names of the three suppliers you use
most often for concrete. Then evaluate each company's
performance using this scale:

A = The Best
B = Above Average
C = Average, Same As Their Competition
D = Needs Improvement
F = Terrible
N = No Opinion

Write in Supplier's Name You Use Most Often

Write in Your 2nd Most Often Used Suplier's Name

Write in Your 3rd Most Often Used Suplier's Name

Overall Product Quality:
Concrete Workability
Concrete Pumpability
Concrete Consistency
Concrete Slump Continuity
Concrete Strength
Concrete Finishability
Concrete Set Time
Overall Customer Service:
Dependable, On Time Delivery
Salesperson Product Knowledge
Driver Courtsey and Skill
Dispatcher Eager to Help
Ordering Convenience
Responsive to Special Needs
Resolves Mistakes Quickly
Price
Billing Accuracy
Credit Terms

-- OVER --

Source: Reprinted with permission, *Inc.* magazine, May 1991. Copyright 1991 by Goldhirsh Group,
Inc., 38 Commercial Wharf, Boston, MA 02110.

Says Franceschi, "We have a strong belief that if something is worth doing, it's probably worth measuring. This is a way for us to sound an alarm if something is not right."[2]

By using its surveys to develop high-quality products, and backing them up with high-quality service (as defined by customers), Granite Rock is able to charge 6 percent more than its toughest competitors. As a result of its outstanding performance, this relatively small industry player has been attracting the attention of small and large competitors throughout the world, who visit Watsonville to learn more about Granite Rock's success.

Customer Visits

There are many ways to find out what is most important to your customers, and the very best technique for gathering information about your customers is to visit them.

All owners and managers of SMM firms should visit at least some of their MVCs twice a year. Sitting in the customer's office and not being in control of the meeting is a humbling learning experience that almost magically leads to better decisions. It is amazing what you will learn if you just show up and listen.

*   *   *   *   *

It takes good communication skills to stay in touch with customers' wants and needs. Unfortunately, few owners and managers of SMMs know how to interview customers and probe for the information they need in order to improve their products and services. Chapter 3 will outline the basics of customer interviews.

KEY POINT

Knowing more about your customers' wants and needs and developing systematic methods of soliciting their opinions is the first essential step toward developing a successful business marketing program.

SUGGESTED ACTION

Select three or four of your Most Valuable Customers and send them copies of the acid test. If their ratings are significantly different from yours, request a personal interview to find out why.

NOTES

1. Personal interview with the author, December 5, 1992.
2. Edward O. Welles, "How're We Doing?," *Inc.* magazine, May 1991, p. 80.

Chapter Three

The Customer Interview
A Simple but Powerful Tool

Because determining customer needs and wants is so vital, the ability to interview customers, in person and by telephone, is a critical skill of the business marketer. Unfortunately, though most general marketing books stress the importance of gathering detailed information about customers, they don't describe how to go about it. Interviewing skills may be covered in detail in academic texts on marketing research, but they are too technical to interest the typical owner or manager of the small or midsize manufacturing firm.

This chapter will outline some basic interviewing techniques that anyone can use to gather important customer information. These techniques require *no previous background or experience in conducting interviews.*

There is nothing mysterious about the interviewing process. Gathering information from customers, prospective employees, subordinates, and superiors is something that successful owners and managers of SMMs do every day. With a few simple techniques and a minimum of practice, these everyday conversations can be turned into powerful marketing tools.

THE UNSTRUCTURED INTERVIEW

One simple but effective technique for gathering customer information is the nondirective, or unstructured, interview. Instead of asking questions in a rigid order, nondirective interviews include a simple checklist of questions that can be asked in any order. The interviewer has the flexibility to change the course of the conversation when resistance is sensed, or to pursue topics that have elicited a positive response.

One benefit of the unstructured interview is that it is informal; it creates a relaxed atmosphere that encourages the respondent to open up. For this technique to be effective, though, the interviewer must be adept at steering the conversation in the most meaningful direction in order to get the needed information from the respondent.

To be a good interviewer, you must have or develop a keen interest in what motivates other people. You must become something of a psychologist, at least for the duration of the interview. You must be objective; you must open your mind to opinions, views, and information that might be contradictory to your own views or experience. This is difficult for many successful entrepreneurs and managers who believe they have all the right answers and who have difficulty in shedding their strong opinions and biases.

The unstructured interview can produce ideas, comments, and important pieces of marketing information that would be difficult to uncover by any other method. For example: I once secured a lunchtime interview with an industrial dealer in Phoenix, Arizona, who distributed tractor wear parts. I had been conducting a nationwide survey for a client who was going to invest in a new line of tractor wear parts made in his US foundry. Before he made the investment, he wanted to make sure the market would pay his price.

During our conversation, the dealer casually mentioned that the company he represented had been purchasing its wear parts from a Korean foundry in order to reduce costs. This was a startling revelation. Most people in the industry, including my client, believed that all castings were manufactured in the United States.

Follow-up with other distributors and end users revealed that most major competitors were buying castings from foreign foundries. Price discounting of up to 40 percent was common in the marketplace, and most domestic OEMs were struggling for orders.

I learned more from this lunch conversation than I would have uncovered in three weeks of research work. As a result of the information I gathered from this single interview, my client decided not to invest in the new line of tractor parts, averting a potential new product disaster.

The Personal Interview

The personal interview is the most powerful vehicle for gathering customer information. In a personal interview, you have the opportunity to gain insights and information that you could not solicit in a phone conversation or through a mail survey. I have always been amazed at how much people will tell you in person, and at how much time they will spend in a personal interview, once they've agreed to participate.

Soliciting the Interview

Calling people to obtain personal interviews, particularly if they don't know you, arouses many of the same fears and reservations as a cold call. If you haven't had field sales experience, soliciting interviews can be an intimidating proposition that easily leads to procrastination.

Part of the reason that people may dread soliciting interviews is that they're afraid of being turned down. This fear is largely unfounded; the truth is, most people love to talk about their expertise or to be asked their opinions. You just need to offer them some good reasons why the interview will be worth their time. Here is a suggested approach to use in calling someone to solicit a personal interview:

1. Before you call, think through your introduction and the reasons the respondent should agree to the interview. For example, be prepared to suggest a benefit to the respondent, such as your willingness to share information, or how the information gathered in the interview will help you improve the products and services you sell to the respondent. If necessary, write down your reasons before you make the call.

2. When possible, use a third-party introduction: "I was just talking to Bill Smith [the interviewee's boss], and he suggested that you might be able to help me in my survey on investment castings."

3. Appeal to the person's ego. I noted earlier that most people like to be asked for their opinions or recognized for their expertise. Use this to your advantage in your introduction. Say something like, "I have been searching for someone in the rock crushing industry who really understands cone crusher wear parts, and Jack Johnson mentioned you have a lot of experience in the field."

4. Question the respondent about the best time for an interview. A promised one-hour interview can easily turn into a two-hour interview if the respondent is enjoying the discussion, so schedule it when the respondent will most likely have a large block of time available.

5. Follow up with a confirmation letter. In the letter, confirm the interview date and time, restate the purpose of the interview, and thank the respondent in advance for his or her cooperation. This formalizes and gives credibility to the interview, and also gets the respondent thinking about the subject matter. If necessary, reassure the respondent that the information is confidential and will not be disclosed without his or her permission.

FIGURE 3–1
Personal Interview Checklist

_____	1. Create a friendly atmosphere.
_____	2. State the purpose of the interview.
_____	3. Take notes or tape-record the interview.
_____	4. Start with easy questions.
_____	5. Don't play the role of expert.
_____	6. Avoid the third degree.
_____	7. Allow time for a response.
_____	8. Take advantage of the painful pause.
_____	9. Observe body language.
_____	10. Never show emotion.
_____	11. Don't allow rambling.
_____	12. Listen carefully.
_____	13. Handle sensitive questions sensitively.
_____	14. Offer some information of your own.
_____	15. Stay as long as you are welcome.

You might also consider sending a letter requesting the interview, rather than calling cold. In this letter, you should briefly state the purpose of the interview, tell why you chose the respondent for the interview, and indicate that you will follow up with a phone call to schedule an appointment.

Figure 3–1 presents a 15-point checklist that will help you to prepare for your personal interview. The list includes techniques and suggestions from actual business marketing interviews. The techniques and suggestions are discussed below.[1]

Interviewing Tips

1. Create a friendly, relaxed atmosphere. Controlling tension and creating a relaxed atmosphere are the keys to the success of a personal interview. A general rule is that you must put the respondent at ease before proceeding with the interview.

I often spend the first five minutes of the interview trying to find a common interest that allows me to read the respondent better. For example, in a meeting with a disgruntled customer to discuss quality problems, I commented on a World War II submarine photograph on his desk. The subsequent conversation created a relaxed atmosphere and led to a productive three-hour interview.

It's important to engage in small talk that is of interest to the respondent until he or she is clearly relaxed. It's easy to find a topic of conversation; just look around the room at pictures or other decorations that might suggest something about the respondent's family, hobbies, and so forth.

2. State the purpose of the interview. Make your introduction conversational and tailor it to your usual style and comfort zone. This is crucial; if you don't use your own style, the introduction will sound like a canned speech.

After you've introduced yourself, you may begin with a statement such as this: "Before we spend any more money designing machines for the auto industry, we want to find out what users think of our existing products. We are particularly interested in your thoughts on this subject because of your experience with our type of machinery." Continue to explain the purpose of the interview in as much detail as it takes to put the respondent at ease.

3. Take notes or tape-record the interview. Have your questions well thought out and organized in a checklist. Note taking is generally acceptable during the interview, as long as you don't get preoccupied with your notes and/or lose the respondent's interest.

Tape recorders often intimidate people and can restrict the candor of an interview. However, they ensure that you have a record of precisely what the respondent said. If you wish to tape-record an interview, always ask in advance for the respondent's permission, and assure the respondent that the tape will be used only for the purposes of the interview. If there is hesitancy, volunteer to provide the respondent with a transcript of the interview so that he or she can make corrections or additions. (This is a way to get additional, possibly valuable, information.) If there is still hesitancy, drop the idea, and simply take notes.

4. Start with easy questions. Establish rapport by discussing points of agreement early in the interview; save the tough questions for later. Begin with open-ended questions that are easily answered, such as, "What is your opinion on why the market for bronze castings is declining?" If possible, compliment the respondent on his or her knowledge (but don't be phony or manipulative).

5. Don't play the role of expert (even if you are). Make sure you do not patronize your respondent by playing the role of expert. Do not interject your opinions into the interview. Be neutral, even if your credentials are better than the respondent's.

6. Avoid the third degree. Avoid third-degree questions that make you sound like a police interrogator; this approach may lead to an outright refusal to answer. Avoid blunt questions or commands such as, "We want specific data on that problem." Instead, use softer phrases such as, "Perhaps you could explain . . . " or "Can you explain what you meant by . . . " or "Could I ask you a couple of questions about that situation . . . ?"

7. Allow time for a response. Give the respondent time to answer each question. Don't leap in and rescue him or her if there is a pause. Many people like to take plenty of time to think through an answer.

8. Take advantage of the painful pause. You can use silence to your advantage in an interview. Most respondents are afraid of silent periods during an interview and will attempt to fill the gap by elaborating on their answers or supplying other information. Be patient and wait them out. This technique is particularly useful when you are asking sensitive questions. The pressure to fill the silence sometimes causes respondents to give out proprietary information they would not otherwise disclose.

9. Observe body language. Observe physical actions, such as negative facial expressions, a twinkle in the eyes, tone of voice, fidgeting, hand waving, looking away, an impulsive smile, and other physical evidence of emotion (positive or negative) or rising tension levels. Awareness of body language will enable you to control the course of the interview, redirecting a question if you've touched a nerve or probing further if the respondent seems interested.

Some people simply cannot tune into body language. This seems to be a particular problem for technical professionals and others who like to view the world in terms of mathematical equations. Men generally seem to have more difficulty in reading body language than women do. If you are weak in this crucial skill, developing it will be worth your while, and you may need the help of someone who *is* adept at reading body language. You might also find some help in popular psychology books.

10. Never show emotion.   Respondents will be sensitive to your emotions and may sometimes unconsciously begin modifying their answers in order to accommodate you. Never show your feelings (whether acceptance or disapproval) about a response, because this may bias the rest of the answers you get.

To get into the neutral or objective role, I find it helps if I pretend to be a psychiatrist who is about to interview someone with a serious mental health problem. When I am questioning the respondent, I become more animated and friendly, in order to encourage the interviewee to open up. When I listen to responses, I am attentive, but I don't show any emotion so that the answer won't be biased by my reaction.

11. Don't allow rambling.   When some people get nervous or want to change the subject, they tend to fill the time interval with idle chitchat. If this happens during an interview, either ask a new question or politely say something like "Would you mind if we got back to the question of competitor pricing for just a minute?"

12. Listen carefully.   The interviewer must develop a high level of listening skills in order to be successful. This is much more difficult than it sounds. Most people are poor listeners. While they should be paying attention to what is being said, they are thinking about what they want to say next.

To get the most out of a personal interview, it's vital to listen carefully and probe when necessary. For example, if a respondent said, "Your new product looks good, but it isn't what we need for our production line," you might probe further by asking, "What exactly do you need for the line?" Another approach is to repeat the respondent's answer to confirm the meaning. For example, "Earlier you answered that production needs to increase by 1,000 tons. Do you mean 1,000 tons per week?"

During an interview, respondents may drop hints, whisper things, mention personal problems, refer to political and communication problems, and generally offer many clues about what is going on around them or how they feel. With practice, you will begin to recognize these important clues and learn to respond appropriately. Many opportunities to gather hard-to-get information present themselves when you develop excellent listening skills.

13. Handle sensitive questions sensitively.   Some of the information you request may be considered proprietary and will trigger a negative reaction from the respondent. If you sense this happening, you can back off and switch to a different question to lower the tension. Or you might restate the question in a different and less threatening form.

One useful technique is rephrasing the question so that it requires a yes or no response, or an estimate rather than a hard figure. Instead of asking how many machines are produced per year, say, "We estimate that you produce 550 machines in an average year. Is that a reasonable figure?" Or ask, "Is your employment in the 100 to 150 range?" This allows the respondent to give you the information you want without feeling that anything of a proprietary nature has been disclosed.

Don't be afraid to ask the question. The respondent will signal you if the answer is sensitive.

14. Offer some information of your own.   Before ending the interview, ask the respondent whether there is anything you can tell him or her. In my experience, the person will often come back with a question about a competitor. My personal rule is to answer any questions the respondent poses as candidly as he or she answered mine. However, I never divulge proprietary information about competitors. This helps to reinforce the facts that I am honest and that the interview was worth the respondent's time.

15. Stay as long (but only as long) as you are welcome.   Try to remain in the interview as long as the respondent is willing to talk. However, if he or she begins looking at the clock or reminds you there are only five minutes left, choose the most important question to end the interview. Don't overstay your welcome.

THE TELEPHONE INTERVIEW

Since face-to-face contacts are expensive, especially if conducted over a large geographic area, developing good telephone interviewing skills is important. The biggest advantage of the telephone interview is that it allows for wide geographical coverage at high speed and low cost.

The telephone is well suited for interviews that require responses that are simple or can be quantified, or answers to a few important technical questions that might establish the basis for a follow-up letter or a personal interview. Unless you plan to tape the interview (which is rarely done by small manufacturers), the telephone is not an effective vehicle for asking

FIGURE 3–2
Telephone Interviewing Guidelines

---

1. Have your questions and supplies ready before you call.
2. Be prepared to state your purpose.
3. Don't disguise your identity.
4. If possible, use a third-party introduction.
5. If you don't know the person to call, aim higher rather than lower.
6. Get the respondent's name quickly.
7. Be prepared to reach voice mail.
8. Be prepared for rude replies.
9. When in doubt, ask the tough questions.
10. Leave the door open for follow-up questions.

THE REPORTER'S OATH

If the person you called won't tell you
what you need to know, then you
have simply called the wrong person.

                              CALL SOMEONE ELSE!

---

questions that require a lot of time to answer, or for exploring attitudes and opinions. Even if you tape interviews, respondents will be less willing to spend long periods of time on the phone than they would in a personal interview.

Preparing for the Interview

To ensure that you get the maximum return from your telephone interview, you need to do a little preparation. You can save time and money by studying the checklist in Figure 3–2 before you make your call. The items in the checklist are discussed below.

1. Have questions and supplies ready before you call. Write down every question you want to get an answer to, in simple form. (Remember, you don't have to ask the questions in a rigid order.)

Have paper, pens, and cassette tapes (to use in recording your thoughts after the interview) ready to use. It is helpful to dictate the answers you receive after each call, to save time and to record the information while it's fresh in your mind.

2. Be prepared to state your purpose.   Think of how you will succinctly express your purpose to the respondent. Write it down.

3. Don't disguise your identity.   Do not assume false identities. It is not worth the risk and may ultimately backfire, when your true identity is discovered. (Remember that some of the prospects you phone may become customers in the future.) You can usually get the information you need by using honest and legitimate interview methods.

4. If possible, use a third-party introduction.   If you are networking within a company, always use the names you pick up as referrals. Say, "The [president] suggested you may be able to help me."

5. If you don't know the person to call, aim higher rather than lower.   If you want to interview the person in the company who does the purchasing of widgets, but you don't have a specific name, call the company and ask for the appropriate department or title of the person. I usually ask for the customer service department; this department is generally helpful and will probably know the appropriate person or persons to interview.

When in doubt about whom to interview, aim higher rather than lower. For example, if you need to speak to someone in the sales department, contact the senior marketing employee, perhaps the vice president of sales. If this person is not the correct contact, he or she can refer you down the chain of command. However, if you start lower, you will seldom be referred to a more senior person.

A word of advice: Gatekeepers—receptionists, secretaries, and so forth—are trained to screen calls. Don't try to manipulate them or otherwise alienate them, because they have considerable power and you may need their help in the future. Like anyone else, they will respond to honesty, respect, and courtesy. Ask for their names, write them down, remember them, and use them. You might also try to ask questions they cannot answer and politely ask to be referred to someone who can answer.

6. Get the respondent's name quickly. The respondent's attention will be riveted for 15 seconds after he or she says "Hello." Make sure you get the person's name, and use it before every key point. Write it down, so you will get it right.

7. Be prepared to reach voice mail. Some people are seldom at their desks or always seem to be in meetings. This is particularly true in large corporations where voice mail is commonly used. Usually, you will have the option of speaking with a secretary or a receptionist if you don't want to leave a voice mail message. In most cases I recommend taking the option of speaking to someone, because you can find out whether the person you want is away from his or her desk or on a two-month sabbatical. When the secretary or receptionist comes on the line, ask when is the best time to call or how else you might locate the respondent.

8. Be prepared for rude replies. Use patience and tact. Be ready with a reply in the event you receive a rude response. A typical response is, "I don't have time to talk to researchers." You might reply, "This will only take a few minutes, and I think you might find it interesting because we are looking for ways to make your job easier." As an alternative, ask if you can call back at a more convenient time.

9. When in doubt, ask the tough questions. After you have established rapport with the respondent, don't be afraid to ask sensitive questions. Soften tough questions with qualifying words such as "perhaps" or "maybe," or rephrase them—for example, "From what you have said, it appears that XVC Company has half of this market. Is that about right?" Be prepared to redirect the question if you get a negative response.

10. Leave the door open for follow-up questions. Always keep the door open at the end of the interview. Ask if you can call back if you happen to think of another question for the respondent. Very few people will refuse this request, especially if your tone is polite and you have shown respect for the respondent's knowledge and time.

Example of a Telephone Interview

Following is a hypothetical example of a telephone interview conducted by Ben Williams, the owner of Hi-Speed Machines, a small manufacturing firm. Ben wants to gather information from prospective end users of a new product his firm is considering developing. This is a pilot inquiry to determine the best candidates for subsequent in-depth personal interviews. Another objective is to find out the trend in production speeds, the weaknesses of competitive designs, and the service problems his competitors encounter.

Receptionist:

Good morning. Delectable Foods.

Ben:

Hello, this is Ben Williams calling. Can you tell me who in engineering specifies new equipment purchases?

Receptionist:

Well, I am not quite sure, but Mr. Edgington is the director of engineering.

Ben:

Is he in today? [She says yes.] Good. Before you connect me, can you tell me his direct-dial number in case I lose him?

[*The receptionist gives Ben the number and then connects him.*]

Prospect:

George Edgington.

Ben:

Hello, Mr. Edgington, this is Ben Williams of Hi-Speed Machines. I am doing a survey on high-speed case packers. Is there anyone in your organization who has a lot of experience in installing and maintaining XYZ case packers?

George:

Well, that would probably be Jim Johnson. He was the one who managed the installation of the XYZ machines and is in charge of that whole production line.

[*Ben gets the number and calls Jim Johnson.*]

Prospect:

Jim Johnson.

Ben:

Hello, Mr. Johnson, this is Ben Williams of Hi-Speed Machines. Mr. Edgington suggested I call you. He said you were the expert on high-speed case packers.

Jim:

Well, I don't know about that, but I certainly have spent a lot of time making them run.

Ben:

Jim, my company manufactures case packers, and we are developing a new high-speed machine for juice lines. Before we spend a lot of money on development, we want to get the opinions of users who have a lot of experience with this type of machine. Could I ask you a few questions?

Jim:

Uh . . . how long will it take? I have a meeting to go to.

Ben:

I just have a few questions, and am very interested in what you think about future production speeds.

Jim:

When you say high speed, what range are you talking about?

[The interview progresses to a question about the company's production line speeds, which is proprietary information.]

Ben:

Jim, how fast do you run the juice line during a typical shift?

Jim:

Well, you know, the company considers that proprietary information, because it relates to output.

Ben:

Yes, but we need to get some idea of your requirements so that we can design a machine with enough capability to handle your future production speeds. We are thinking about speeds up to 80 cases per minute (cpm).

Jim:

Wow! That is pretty ambitious.

Ben:

Would a range of 60 to 70 cpm be adequate to cover your future production needs?

Jim:

Anything above 65 cpm would be adequate.

[The interview progresses to a sensitive question.]

Ben:

Jim, have you had any problems with the XYZ packer? Any service or design problems that caused downtime?

Jim:

Well, uh. . . .

[Now is the time to take advantage of the painful pause. This is sensitive information, and Jim must think through how he will respond to the question.]

Jim:

> There *have* been some problems with controls, . . . and the damn erector mechanism breaks if you go over 40 cpm. It takes two weeks to get an erector bar, which just killed our June production schedule.

[Now it's time to close the interview.]

Ben:

> Well, I don't want to take up too much of your time, and I know you need to get to your meeting. Would you mind if we brought our prototype drawings of the new packer over sometime? We would sure like your and your staff's opinions about the new model, and any ideas you may have on how to build it so that you don't experience the same service problems.

Jim:

> Sure. Just give me a call at least a week in advance, and I'll set something up.

Ben:

> OK. Thanks a lot for your help. I will give you a call next week.

In the example above, Jim readily agreed to the telephone interview. Here's how Ben might have handled the conversation if Jim did not want to talk on the phone:

Jim:

> Uh . . . I am really busy and don't have time to discuss case packers right now.

Ben:

> Jim, I am sure you are a busy man. Is there a possibility we could have lunch next week, or could I get just 10 minutes of your time before or after working hours?

Another variation:

Jim:

> I really don't have the time, but if I spend time talking to you, what do I get out of it?

Ben:

> I only have a couple of questions to ask you, and I won't take very long. We know you use high-speed case packers and thought you might be interested in helping us develop a machine that could increase your line speeds to over 70 cpm.

Jim:

You mean *70 cases a minute?*

Jim is now hooked, and will likely continue the conversation or schedule a time when they can talk later.

* * * * *

Interviewing customers is an essential tool of business marketing, a skill that anyone can learn with a minimum of training and practice. Perhaps the most demanding use of interviewing skills is in gathering information about competitors and markets—the subject of Chapter 4.

KEY POINT

Basic interviewing skills are crucial to success in business marketing. Anyone who is in regular contact with customers and prospects needs to develop basic interviewing skills. Simple interviewing techniques can easily be learned on the job and applied immediately.

SUGGESTED ACTION

The next time you need to gather important information from someone on the telephone, take a couple of minutes and review the 10 steps in Figure 3–2. After the call, review the points again to see what you did right and wrong. If you are serious about improving your interviewing skills, ask a friend to listen to your phone interview and evaluate your performance.

NOTES

1. Some of the ideas included in this checklist were drawn from Aubrey Wilson, *The Assessment of Industrial Markets,* (London: Hutchinson, 1968), pp. 164–198, and Paul N Hague, *The Industrial Market Research Handbook* (New York: Franklin Watts, 1988).

Chapter Four

How to Gather Competitive and Market Intelligence
Easy, Cost-Effective Strategies

Now that you have developed a detailed profile of your customers, the next steps in business marketing are to prepare a profile of your competitors and to learn how to monitor your markets. In the past, it was possible to be successful without spending much time studying competitors and markets. Even today, most SMMs don't bother to develop a systematic means of gathering competitive and market intelligence. Instead, they rely on their intuitive feelings about the competition and the marketplace, and some have managed to survive quite well without spending much time collecting hard data.

However, because of rapid change and greatly increased competition (especially international competition), developing a method of monitoring competitors and markets on an ongoing basis is becoming crucial, not only for success but for *survival.* Today it's vital for manufacturing firms to keep tabs on what the competition is doing, particularly in terms of new products and services.

The payoffs from gathering competitive and market intelligence on a regular basis can be immediate, such as winning a specific bid, capturing a customer account, or improving the marketability of a product, or they can be longer-term, such as increasing your market share over a period of years.

To demonstrate the importance of competitive intelligence, let's begin with the story of how Action Machinery, a small manufacturer with big ideas, took on an industry giant and won, thanks to spending a small amount of time on investigating the primary competitor.

DAVID VERSUS GOLIATH—THE CASE OF ACTION MACHINERY

Hal Hickman, a Portland, Oregon, businessman, recognized a weakness in a competitor company that dominated the market for hydraulic manipulators (large, robot-like machines). His decision to pit his company, Action Machinery, against the legendary giant, General Electric (GE), seemed like financial suicide.

But Hickman had a hunch that smallness might be an advantage in the design and manufacture of manipulators that could effortlessly pick up 10,000-pound loads of hot castings in a foundry. The ingenious mechanical hands of the manipulator could save hundreds of man-hours and eliminate dangerous risks by doing the dirty work of cleaning the sand from hot castings and knocking off the stubborn pouring spouts. Men with sledge hammers had done the job before GE designed a machine to eliminate the human chore.

The problem with GE's machine was its high cost, which prevented many companies from buying it. GE's rigid pricing policies only exacerbated the problem.

An Oregon foundry which needed but couldn't afford the GE manipulator asked Hickman's company to adapt one of its traditional knuckle-boom cranes to manipulate castings. Hickman was intrigued. He wondered if it would be possible to build a competitive model patterned on the traditional crane at a price foundries could afford.

Hickman collected every bit of intelligence he could find about GE's manipulators and strategies. His company gathered pricing data from purchasing agents. From foundry maintenance people he discovered the problems and drawbacks of the GE models. His employees worked long hours to create a detailed profile of the giant competitor, and Hickman even asked a third party to interview GE management for more product and market information.

In the end, Action Machinery designed a machine that was rugged, dependable, and versatile, and that could be offered at a lower price than GE's product. So successful was Action's manipulator that GE eventually closed down its US operation and Action took over as the leader in the field, proving that a small company can be a formidable competitor when it takes advantage of competitive intelligence.

As the story of Action Machinery illustrates, SMMs have some tremendous advantages over larger competitors, if they do their competitive intelligence homework. Unfortunately, in my experience, the owners and managers of most small manufacturing firms make major decisions every day based on little more than intuition or "gut feel." Many of these decisions end up as costly mistakes. Gathering competitive intelligence can help to reduce the risk of making such mistakes.

THE COMPETITIVE MATRIX

How much do you know about *your* competitors? Developing a competitive matrix is a quick way for you to find out what you know about your direct competitors, in terms of several critical success factors. By filling in the matrix, you will begin to recognize the strengths and weaknesses of your competitors, and to identify areas of existing or potential competitive advantage for your firm.

A typical competitive matrix for SMMs is presented in Figure 4–1. The answers to the following questions are included in the matrix. (Refer to the circled numbers in the matrix as you work through the list below.)

1. How many direct competitors are there for your product or service, and what product line or model are you comparing?
2. Who are the top three or four competitors? List them, and note their locations.
3. Determine the company size—estimate each competitor's size in terms of sales volume and number of employees.
4. Indicate the specific models or product lines that your product competes with. You may want to do a matrix for each model to ensure that you are comparing apples to apples.
5. List the most recent bid or selling price, including discounts, of each competitor's product.
6. Indicate the type of distribution used by each competitor—whether it sells its product via direct sales, manufacturer's reps, distributors, dealers, or other channels.
7. Describe the time needed for delivery in terms of days or months.
8. Rate customer service and support, on a scale of 1 (poor) to 10 (excellent).
9. Rate overall product quality, also on a scale of 1 to 10.

Now that you've seen an example of a competitive matrix, it's time to develop one of your own. Choose a specific product or model, and select

FIGURE 4–1
The Competitive Matrix (*Known Competitors: Four; Your Product: Model 1060*)

① Direct competitors: Product line:

② Company and Location	③ Company Size*	④ Model or Product No.	⑤ Selling Price	⑥ Type of Distribution	⑦ Time Needed for Delivery	⑧ Service†	⑨ Quality†
ABC Inc. Hope, NM	$5 million (?)	16d	$125,000	Direct	150	8	7
Plat Co Angus, CA	$10 million 100	25B	(?)	Reps	120	6	5
EG Inc. Syracuse, NY	(?) 450	900	$180,000	Direct	180	4	7
Posimate Gahanna, OH	$1 million (?)	M40	$78,000	Reps	120	4	5

*Sales dollars and number of employees.

†Estimated on a scale of 1 (poor) to 10 (excellent).

three or four of your direct competitors. Prepare a competitive matrix similar to the one in Figure 4–1, without spending any additional time researching your answers.

If you find that your competitive matrix has a lot of blank spaces, don't worry. The rest of this chapter will help you to develop your competitive intelligence system and fill in the blanks.

THE CUSTOMERS' PERCEPTIONS

The next and perhaps the most important competitive question to ask is, How do your products and services compare to those of your competitors, *from the customers' point of view?* All manufacturers have strong intuitive feelings about how they compare to competitors at the point of sale. They spend considerable time and money in developing and refining products based on their own perception of competitors. However, seldom do small manufacturers take the next step, finding out what the person who really counts—the customer—thinks about them and their products.

Here is a quick way to find out how your customers perceive your company, its products and services: Choose one of your strongest competitors—a competitor who will be bidding against you in the future for the business of one of your MVCs. From the competitive matrix you developed earlier, choose three or four factors that you feel will be critical in winning the order from this MVC. (If you aren't sure which critical factors to use, choose delivery, price, product quality, and sales and support.) List these factors on the form in Figure 4–2 and ask the MVC to rate you against one or two competitors on a scale of 1 to 5 (5 is the highest or best score).

To develop an even better idea of how you compare to an important competitor, ask three or four more of your MVCs to rate you, using the form in Figure 4–2. If you don't feel comfortable asking customers to complete this brief form, have a third party, or perhaps a market research professional, do it for you.

It is often an eye-opening experience to find out your customers' perceptions. I conducted this exercise for a robot manufacturer I'll call Allied Manufacturing, during a period when a foreign competitor, Robot International, was trying to penetrate the US market. My client's assumption was that its product quality and service, though they weren't great, were acceptable to most customers. This assumption was based entirely on

FIGURE 4–2

Ask a Customer (*How Do We Compare to the Competitors?*)

List below three or four factors that you feel are critical in getting an order or retaining a customer. Ask important customers to give you a grade on a scale of 1 to 5 (1 is poor, 3 is average, and 5 is excellent).

	Critical Factors	Your Company	Competitor 1	Competitor 2
1.	_____	_____	_____	_____
2.	_____	_____	_____	_____
3.	_____	_____	_____	_____
4.	_____	_____	_____	_____

what people within the company wanted to believe; no one had ever bothered to ask customers directly.

Nor was anyone in the company interested in soliciting input from customers, until the foreign robot manufacturer suddenly appeared in the US market and the company began losing orders. Then I was asked to conduct a customer survey for the company.

I interviewed people at both of Allied's MVCs, who explained in detail why they switched to the competitor. During my interviews, I found that the critical factors were price, quality, delivery, and service after the sale. Some of these MVCs rated the foreign manufacturer significantly higher on several critical success factors, as shown in Figure 4–3.

Follow-up interviews with the MVCs revealed that they both felt Allied's quality and service were very poor and did not justify the high price the company was charging for its machines. They felt so strongly, in fact, that both had decided to purchase the foreign competitor's product and felt that more competition was necessary in the US market. Within months, the foreign competitor had developed a foothold in the United States and had begun taking even more orders away from my client.

The lesson is simple: the small manufacturer that hopes to succeed in the face of growing competition must have a clear, detailed understanding of how it compares to competitors in the eyes of the customer.

FIGURE 4–3
Allied Manufacturing versus Robot International (*Customer Ratings*)

Critical Success Factor	Allied Manufacturing	Robot International
1. Delivery	3	3
2. Quality	1	4
3. Price	3	5
4. Service	1	4

The customers described the two critical factors in the following terms:

Service:	Product quality:
Response to problems	Factory testing
Success of field fixes	Production downtime
Emergency parts delivery	Installation problems
Design solutions	Annual maintenance costs

Note: Ratings were made on a scale of 1 to 5:
   1 = Poor
   3 = Average
   5 = Excellent

Gathering Competitive Intelligence: A Simple Case Study

Managers of small manufacturing companies frequently believe that their limited financial resources prevent them from doing much to discover their competitors' intentions or capabilities. However, a good deal of competitive information is either free or can be acquired for no more than the cost of a phone call, photocopies, or the time spent in finding the information. In addition, many of the research techniques required to find the information are fairly simple and can be easily learned.

In 1973, I was hired by the general marketing manager of a large forest products company to conduct a "quick and dirty" research project on manufacturers of polyvinyl chloride (PVC) building products, such as siding and baseboards, used in home building and remodeling. The company was already committed to building a $50 million PVC, or plastics, manufacturing plant, despite the fact that no one in the company knew much about the competition.

The general marketing manager was in a spot, because time and budget constraints would not allow implementation of a well-thought-out research project. I had just 30 days to gather the needed competitive information and provide the manager with some direction before he met with his superiors to discuss the plant.

In an annual buyer's guide to the plastics industry, found at the local library, I looked up the names and phone numbers of all known suppliers of PVC products in the United States. I decided to be bold and call every company.

When using the phone to probe for information, I find it best to start with people who like to talk. I called the sales managers of the companies and told them I was a consultant on retainer from a large forest products company and that I was looking for information on the PVC siding market.

I always begin such conversations with easy-to-answer questions about the marketplace, or an open-ended question such as "How would I go about finding a competitor in the industry who may want to be acquired?" Depending on the level of the respondents' receptivity, I move toward the harder questions, such as the size of companies in the industry, or selling prices.

The number one rule of phone networking is never to end a conversation without getting two additional names of people who are well known within the industry, and if possible, their phone numbers. While networking, I happened to reach a sales manager in a small PVC siding manufacturer who had recently offered his resignation and was shopping for a job at his competitors' plants. This person had been in the industry for many years and had worked for several companies in production, sales, and engineering jobs.

We hit it off right from the start. I was a consultant trying to find competitive information for a new company coming into the industry. He needed a job and was eager to know about the new competitor and about potential opportunities at competitive companies. I promised to buy him dinner when I went through North Carolina on my "whirlwind" intelligence survey, and suggested that I would share any of the competitive information I had gathered and maybe even offer some insight into which companies were the best potential employers.

The dinner turned out to be the most productive two hours of the entire project. This person knew the strengths and weaknesses of all the major competitors in the industry. He gave me many hard-to-get details about competitive pricing and product costs—details which showed that many competitors were not making any money.

The next day we resumed our discussion. I interviewed him about industry channels of distribution, manufacturing strengths, promotion techniques, and a host of other competitive factors. The interview revealed that many of the companies within the PVC industry used specialized reps and dealers to sell products directly to consumers in major cities, which required telemarketing, local advertising, and constant price discounting. This was important information, since my client's organization marketed only through established distribution centers at wholesale prices, and its buyers were dealers, not consumers.

My final report revealed that the marketing channels, competitive prices, discounts, and selling techniques used by the leading competitors were totally different from the system used by my client. My conclusion was that there would be little chance for the client to compete without a major organizational and strategy change.

The entire competitive intelligence project took less than six weeks to complete and was accomplished on a very small budget, using the telephone and one intense week in the field doing personal interviews.

AN EIGHT-STEP COMPETITIVE INTELLIGENCE PROGRAM

Occasional last-minute guerrilla intelligence excursions like this one are really not the best way to monitor competitors' activities. Even though this project generated considerable information in a short time, it was almost too late to avert an expensive disaster. What is really needed is an ongoing, do-it-yourself approach to gathering competitive intelligence, one that can be carried out by your own employees.

Before we get started, though, a word about ethics: *Competitive intelligence,* as I use the term, focuses on the legal gathering of public or private information about competitors. Illegal theft of information and spying are not valid competitive intelligence methods and are *wrong.* Espionage techniques, varying from misrepresentation to bribery to outright theft, are used by some companies. These techniques are illegal and can bring severe penalties.

Ironically, espionage and other unethical methods are not necessary or warranted. A company can be highly competitive without stooping to illegal and unethical activities.

Discussed below are eight steps you can take to develop an effective and ethical competitive intelligence program for your company.

Step 1: Hire a part-time researcher.   Assign the task of collecting data and locating sources of information to a part-time researcher. (A business school student is an ideal candidate for the job.)

The researcher's job will be to gather competitive information from designated sources and from other people in the company. The researcher should create a competitor intelligence file and pass along information, as it is received, to the appropriate managers in the organization, who will be responsible for evaluating the data on a regular basis. (An evaluation process will be discussed in detail in Step 8—see page 69— and is one example of how to use information.)

Step 2: Acquire competitive literature.   Acquire competitors' literature and price lists on an ongoing basis. Simply call their sales departments, which are usually willing to provide this information to anyone who requests it. If you don't get what you need from a company's sales department, try its customer service department, which has a focus on being helpful to outsiders. (You might ask a third party to call for this competitive information, if you are uncomfortable making such calls.)

Step 3: Buy competitive products.   If the competitive product is small and relatively inexpensive, buy one and take it apart to see how it works. If you manufacture large, capital products, try to visit a customer's plant to see competitive products in operation.

I once visited a customer who was so unhappy with the performance of a machine he had bought from a competitor that he pointed out every weak point in the design and backed it up with failure data and downtime figures. We immediately used the data in our own new product designs and trained our salespeople to take advantage of the weaknesses we had discovered in the competitor's product.

Step 4: Train field salespeople.   Field salespeople can gather feedback on competitors if they know how and what to ask for. Salespeople regularly get to see competitive products in the plants where they are performing, often get to see competitors' bids and pricing, and regularly hear complaints about competitor's weaknesses from buyers. Enlist their support by introducing the subject of competitive intelligence at the next sales meeting, and by telling reps specifically what information you need.

Step 5: Get senior managers involved.   Assign key managers the task of going out and talking with customers twice every year about

FIGURE 4–4
Low-Cost Information Sources

1. Directories of manufacturers.
2. Yellow pages.
3. Competitive advertising.
4. Competitors' employment ads.
5. Clipping services.
6. Competitors.
7. Suppliers.
8. Distributors and agents.
9. Computerized information services.
10. Competitor stock.
11. Labor agreements.
12. UCC filings.
13. Court records.
14. Tax records.
15. Credit firms.
16. Patent information.
17. Industry gurus.
18. Reference librarians.

competitors' products and services. Make sure the customers they visit have also purchased the competitor's products. They will then be in a position to compare your products with the others they have used.

Step 6: Use low-cost information sources. Keep a permanent file of all competitor information, no matter how trivial it may appear. Individual pieces of data may not tell you much, but when a collection of information is evaluated over time, it may give you a clear picture of the competition.

A few of the low-cost information sources that can provide useful pieces of the competitive puzzle are listed in Figure 4–4 and described below.

1. Manufacturing company directories. Every state publishes a directory of manufacturers, listing their names, addresses, and phone numbers, and including information on sales volume, product standard industrial classification (SIC) codes, and number of employees. Directories of all states can usually be found in larger city and county libraries.

The Dun & Bradstreet *Million Dollar Directory,* which was cited in Chapter 2 as a source of customer information, can also be used to find information about your competitors. The directory comes in two volumes. The first contains information on companies with a net worth of $1 million or more. The second volume lists information on companies that are valued between $500,000 and $999,000. The *Dun's Business Identification Service* is a microfiche listing of 10 million companies and includes many businesses below $500,000 in value. The *Thomas Register of Manufacturers* lists 123,000 manufacturers by products, city, and state. All these directories can be found in any large city library, or in university libraries.

By using some of these directories as well as state manufacturing directories and computerized association lists of member companies, I was able to find the size (number of employees), sales volume, SIC codes, and names and titles of executives of 10 very small companies that manufactured single-board computer products.

2. Yellow pages. The yellow pages has a good description of the trading area of a competitor, or its channels of distribution—sales reps, agents, distributors, and dealers. You can access the yellow pages of many cities in any large public library. In many cities across the nation, you can access the *Electronic Yellow Pages* through DIALOGUE, an on-line computer service.

3. Competitive advertising. A simple and frequently overlooked source of competitive information is your competitors' ads. Make sure you get on the mailing lists of all trade journals related to your market segments. Assign someone to cut out all competitor ads, product releases, and stories in these journals. By keeping a tally of all advertising, you can determine the relative size of your competitors' ad budget and which market segments they are pursuing. In many cases, you can call the editor of the journal in which the ads were placed and get a tally of inquiries about your competitors' products.

4. Competitor employment ads. Have your part-time researcher monitor all newspapers in which your competitors might run employment ads. This is a good way to monitor hiring patterns. Also, some job descriptions are indicative of changes in strategy.

For example, a while ago a high tech-manufacturer of industrial computer products ran an ad for a programmer with TURBO C and engineering language skills. This was a tip that the company was going to begin developing new products to appeal to new market segments; the company had traditionally designed products using Basic and Assembly.

5. *Clipping services.* Consider paying a monthly fee to a clipping service that will scan newspapers, trade journals, and business publications for articles on your competitors. A local clipping service that covers all daily and weekly newspapers in the states of Oregon and Washington costs $46 per month for five competitors (subjects), plus 35 cents for each clipping in excess of 100 per month.

Most of the articles are about product announcements and good news, but occasionally there are a few lines about a lawsuit or a financial problem that can be followed up through the relevant court or government source. Libraries also collect articles on local companies that are indexed on public databases.

6. *Competitors.* I believe it's important to have a positive relationship with competitors. In trying to gather competitive information, never be shy about being in contact with your competitors or asking them legitimate business questions.

I have always thought it a good idea to know my direct competitors on a first-name basis. When I was a division manager, I always asked for tours of competitors' plants and offered to reciprocate, because I felt that I had an edge in gathering intelligence information. You can learn a great deal about output and capacity by carefully observing the number of employees in the shop, the number and kind of production machines, the number of engineers, and the materials and inventory seen on the tour.

I was a sales manager for a material handling company when I was invited on a tour of our main competitor's plant. During the tour, I discovered that the company was installing commercial programmable logic controllers (PLCs) as machine controls. PLCs are industrial computers that control industrial machines and processing equipment in manufacturing plants. While my company was spending its time and money trying to design its own machine control system, our competitor had purchased a new off-the-shelf commercial system just then coming into the US market.

This information, obtained on a walk through my competitor's plant, turned out to be vital to my company's ability to remain competitive in the marketplace. My company immediately changed to the commercial PLCs even though we had to scrap about $75,000 worth of company-designed controllers. We moved quickly to adopt the new technology into our products, and we found the new controllers solved many service problems. They also provided us with a profitable retrofit capability for customers who needed to convert older controls. An additional bonus was our new ability to bid for the business of Fortune 500 companies which had converted to PLCs.

7. Suppliers. Suppliers know a lot about your competitors and are most likely to supply competitive information if they see the possibility of a sale to your company. For example, a supplier salesman for a European manufacturer of foundry equipment heard rumors that the company he had formerly worked for was having serious cash flow problems. He then discovered from friends employed at the troubled firm that it was on the verge of filing for protection under the Chapter 11 bankruptcy laws. The company was up for sale. He notified his European office, and the president of his company made a bid for the struggling manufacturer.

Supplier salespeople are often the recipients of inside information and fast-breaking rumors. Tell your purchasing office personnel to keep their ears open for information on competitors from garrulous sales reps.

8. Distributors and agents. Distributors and agents are good sources of competitive information because they usually don't owe their allegiance to just one manufacturer; they are independent businesspeople. You simply need to develop a good reason for needing their information. A good time to ask about competitors is when you are interviewing distributors or agents to represent your company.

9. Computerized information services. There are many information services that you can use to retrieve public information on competitors. These services charge anywhere from $100 to more than $300 per hour to access their databases.

However, there are only a few databases with information on companies with less than $5 million in annual sales. Unless you are familiar with computer search techniques and know how to use key words, you might want to get a bid from an information broker. A project I undertook to find basic information on five competitors in the electronics industry with sales under $1 million produced data on three companies and cost about $100 through an information broker.

10.   Competitor stock.   Consider purchasing one share of your top competitors' stock, if the companies are publicly owned. A client that manufactures robots lived in fear of a national robot manufacturer that was a frequent bidder on projects in the investment casting industry. The owner of the smaller company was afraid that his big competitor had the financial resources and marketing muscle to push him out of business. My client's fear of the larger competitor influenced his bid pricing, selling strategies, and product development decisions.

He purchased one share of the larger robot company's stock, a $50 investment. The purchase entitled him to receive the company's annual report and quarterly statements. He was amazed to discover that the big company had lost money in the most recent quarter and showed a history of losses for many years. This was a company with serious financial instability. To make matters worse, it had purchased a hydraulic robot product line from another large robot company, after the market had moved to electric machines. With a new lease on life, my client adopted a more aggressive marketing strategy and never lost another order to the troubled competitor.

11.   Labor agreements.   The US Department of Labor and individual labor unions have copies of labor agreements with specific companies. These agreements contain important information on wage rates, work rules, and contract terms. Probing these agreements can give you insights into your competitors' productivity and costs. This is particularly true of competitors that are union shops. If one of your competitors is a union shop, you can phone its union representative and ask for wage and contract information.

12.   UCC filings.   Most lenders automatically file a Uniform Commercial Code (UCC) form (usually on microfiche) with the state every time a business takes out a loan. Researching UCC documents, which are available to the general public, is an excellent way to find out about your competitors' indebtedness and to gather information on their capital equipment and other assets. In most states, UCC filings are handled by the secretary of state's office.

I obtained a UCC filing on a local machinery manufacturer from the county recording office, which records these filings for real property on a daily basis. You must know the date of a particular transaction to search the recording index, or you can pay a title company to search all county and state records for every filing on the company.

The report I found showed that the company had filings for several bank term loans as well as many short-term contracts, and that it was heavily in debt. This information, combined with complaints from suppliers about slow pay, was a good indication that the company had serious cash flow problems.

13.   Court records.   If your competitive intelligence system reveals that a competitor is involved in a lawsuit, it may be worth your while to look up the public record of the suit. Lawyers fish for information by requesting "all available records" on anything about the company they can think of (whether or not the information appears to be relevant). It is almost inevitable that much of this information (including proprietary information) will end up in the public record.

Product liability court cases against manufacturers are particularly good sources of proprietary information, because the opposing trial lawyers request massive amounts of information. If your competitor is involved in a local court case, you may find it worthwhile to look for the transcript of the trial proceedings. Usually you can find the records by going to the court and telling the court clerk the name of the company, the approximate date of the trial, and whether the case is civil or criminal. Cases are listed alphabetically by company name and year, on microfiche or computer. Be prepared to do a lot of photocopying, because many civil cases on corporations could include hundreds of documents.

14.   Tax records.   Detailed information about competitors' purchased or leased properties, as well as specific tax information, is open to the public. Contact your county tax assessor's office. You can find detailed information on the layout and value of industrial property by simply looking up the company name and business address. Industrial properties are assessed regularly by field reps, and usually there are layout drawings of the property and buildings in the file.

15.   Credit firms.   Dun & Bradstreet, TRW Information Services, and local chapters of the National Association of Credit Managers sell information on the credit-worthiness of companies. Sometimes the reports include information on the backgrounds of the owners and the histories of the companies. The reports include financial information on UCC filings, tax liens, radical sales fluctuations, overdue payables, and net worth, which can give you a good indication of a company's cash flow status. Your local librarian can help you find the addresses and phone numbers of credit firms.

16.   Patent information.   It's vital to get patent information before you design a similar new product, and you don't have to be an engineer to do it. Most states have a patent and trademark depository library, and a number of local affiliates, that will do patent searches for you.

You can call the main patent library in your state, or a local affiliate, and ask for a patent search on a competitor. If you provide the company name and address, most state patent libraries will send you the names and numbers of any patents the firm holds. The cost is usually just the price of the photocopies.

I did this for a client over the phone and received a mail reply that revealed two patent assignments under the company name, the patent number, the year it was issued, the state or country, a classification number, and a brief description of the patent. This information will allow you to do a complete patent search at the library.

In some states you can't get any information by phone; you have to go to the library and do your own patent search. This may take a little time, but the librarian will usually show you how to search if you make an appointment. When you do a search for the complete patent, you have to pay only for the photocopies.

Some states have information clearinghouses, which record on microfiche every patent that has been issued in the state for the last 100 years, and in some cases even longer. Ask your reference librarian to help you find out whether or not your state has such a resource.

Although conducting your own patent search takes a little time, it is far less expensive than hiring a lawyer to defend your company against a patent infringement claim by a competitor.

17.   Industry gurus.   In the many years I've spent as a consultant doing primary research projects for a variety of manufacturing clients, I have always been able to find one person who knows a great deal about a particular industry and its competitors. This could be an engineer with 30 years' experience in the industry, a successful sales manager or sales agency, or even a disgruntled employee looking for another job. This person, whom I call the *industry guru,* can give you volumes of information (much of it from memory) about annual sales, employee turnover, selling prices, discounts, cost advantages, market position, product problems, channel problems, and so forth, on every major company in the industry. For the price of a lunch or a dinner, you can learn more from an industry guru in an hour or two than you might uncover in six months of traditional research.

Not only is the industry guru a wonderful source of competitive information; he or she is also a source for networking and can provide you with other names of people who may have additional information. Gurus can be found by networking on the phone (as described in "Gathering Competitive Intelligence: A Simple Case Study" earlier in this chapter).

18. Reference librarians. Never underestimate the power of a good reference librarian. In addition to the sources listed above, a skilled reference librarian can point you to a variety of other sources of information about your competitors. The most useful reference librarians are the ones associated with business school libraries. If you are not located near a university that has a business school, the reference librarian of the major library in your area is your next best bet.

Step 7: Attend Trade Shows. A piece of the collective intelligence puzzle may fall into your lap if you always have your competitive antennae up and if you make an attempt to be in the right places at the right times. As Woody Allen has pointed out, 80 percent of success in life is simply showing up.

It's useful to attend trade shows regularly. You can often solicit information from competitors at trade shows which they would be reluctant to supply under different circumstances.

In 1989, I was asked by a client to attend a trade show in Germany, at which most of the European manufacturers of manipulators and robots were going to display their machines. My client wanted to penetrate the international market for his products and was considering opening up a European office. The client needed competitive intelligence about a German company that had dominated the European and Asian markets for many years.

During the trade show, the German company announced that it would host a technical discussion, open to the public, in one of the show's meeting rooms. I happened to hear about the meeting from a salesman in the company's booth and made sure I arrived early.

I had expected to slip into the back row and take careful notes of the speeches. The room had enough chairs for 200 guests, but the president of the company, the senior managers, and the company sales force were the only people who showed up. After I got over the shock of the empty room, I decided to take a front-row seat directly in front of the president of the company.

After 15 embarrassing minutes, the president cleared his throat and said, "I am sorry, but there has been a mix-up in the public announcement of our meeting. I apologize for this regrettable oversight, but we will be forced to cancel the meeting." He then asked me who I was and where my company was located. I told him I was a consultant from the United States and was visiting the show to gather information about European machines. He again apologized for the lack of turnout and asked, "How can my company help you?"

I asked him to have someone answer some marketing questions for me. He unhesitatingly appointed one of his bright young employees, a sales engineer who had worked for the company for several years.

The young man was eager to assist me, since he had been directly appointed by the president. We went out for a cup of coffee, and I asked him many questions about the company's production capabilities, engineering philosophy, and market strategy. The information helped me to construct an instant profile of the company, including detailed information about its strengths and weaknesses. The most critical pieces of information I gleaned from this interview were that the company was inflexible when it came to special customer specifications and that it discouraged custom product designs.

Flexibility, innovation, and custom designs were the strengths of my client's company, and when I returned from the show, I assured my client that competing with the market leader was going to be much easier than originally anticipated. The moral of the story: it is amazing what you can discover if you consistently look for competitive information.

Step 8: Hold Periodic Competitive Intelligence Meetings. Once you have the data flowing in on a regular basis, schedule a monthly meeting to review all the information and plan strategies.

One useful technique is the war room approach. Assign specific employees the responsibility for gathering information on specific competitors on a continuous basis. Once a month, have them meet and tape their information on the walls of the meeting room (war room) for everyone to see. This information could include:

- Competitive matrices and information on every competitive product.
- Competitors' literature and prices.

- Copies of competitive advertisements and/or publicity releases.
- Information about competitors' distribution channels.
- Bulleted lists of the features and benefits of competitive products.

The primary tactic in the war room approach is the use of competitive intelligence information to modify products, to change advertising and promotion campaigns, and to modify pricing and channels of distribution strategies. Using this approach, a considerable amount of information can be disseminated in a short period of time. The war room approach makes all employees aware of competition and is an efficient way of monitoring competitors. The approach also ensures a quick response to competitors' moves and shortens the time it takes to build a consensus for decision making.

MONITORING CUSTOMERS AND MARKETS

In addition to knowing your competition, you must understand your markets. You don't need to conduct formal market research to do this. Formal market research, as described in college textbooks, is generally consumer-oriented, formal, and quantitative. It often requires knowledge of sampling techniques and statistics. In my experience, most SMMs who market to other businesses don't do this kind of research. The truth is, it's not necessary or even appropriate for them to do it. The story of Lotus 1-2-3 confirms that it's possible for a small manufacturer to make it big without conducting elaborate, formal quantitative research. As the story goes, while in college at M.I.T. Sloan Business School in the late 1970s, Mitch Kapor submitted a business plan for the company that would become Lotus. The professor gave him only a grade of B because he did not have the statistics to support his market projections.

Kapor had the same problem that many SMMs face: there was no published information on the market, and in his case the market did not yet exist. He made his assumptions based on trends and on "qualitative" information he had gathered from potential customers. Despite the lack of detailed quantitative research, Lotus went on to become the premier spreadsheet company in the country.

One problem with traditional research methods is that they rely on published market information, such as government census data, which is often years old. By the time the data is published, it's out of date—especially in today's fast-changing markets.

Another problem is that most published data is about very large markets or industries. This information will do little for SMMs who market to small niches.

For instance, there is a wealth of census data on the US robot industry but nothing about the small market niche of manipulators (manually operated robots) with over 4,000-pound capacity. Even if the information were available, three-year-old data on the subject is not worth a trip to the library.

Determining Market Size and Growth

For SMMs competing in small market niches, I have found that market size and market share information is hard to get and usually irrelevant. SMMs often occupy niches that are so small and fast-changing that spending money to accurately determine size and share is not warranted.

It is a lot more important to know who the competitors are in each market niche, and especially to have a rough idea of who the top five competitors are, since these will usually account for the biggest piece of the market.

All the SMM really needs to do is to gather enough information to defend its market niches, and to help the company become unique to this customer group. Perhaps the most useful information is simply the total number of plants and customers in a given area that have common needs. If you can develop for your salespeople a reasonably accurate list of the businesses in your territory that are likely prospects, it may be all you need to know about market size.

How much do SMMs need to know about market growth? Very little. Is it possible to determine with any degree of accuracy the growth rates of individual market niches? Probably not. This is another market research problem in which the benefits of knowing probably will not justify the cost of finding out.

What *is* important is to have some feel for whether the industry you sell to is declining or growing. Growth means opportunity, but a declining market means too many competitors, price discounting, reduced margins, and, ultimately, financial disaster—unless the SMM can find another niche. The idea is not to do research and find the exact growth of a particular market segment, but to find out whether you are in an expanding or a contracting industry.

It's possible to get a feel for this by monitoring your own sales records. Carefully plotting sales records of individual products over time and comparing them to other information on changes in the marketplace will give you a rough estimate of growth or decline.

Another simple way of monitoring market growth is to look at industry growth patterns. The federal government publishes an annual directory, *U.S. Industrial Outlook,* which shows the growth rates of all major industries and gives very specific information about factors affecting growth and decline. Because these overall industry growth patterns will have an effect on your particular market niche, monitoring them is important. Other government publications that carry information on industry growth include *Current Industrial Reports, Census of Manufacturers,* and *County Business Patterns.* All these documents can be found in county and university libraries.

Twelve Simple Ways to Gather Market Information

Most SMMs feel that they have a good understanding of their markets. Customers talk to them, the sales force picks up market and customer information, everyone glances at the trade journals, the company is a member of a trade association, and management attends annual trade shows at which everybody who is anybody shows up. What else do they need to know?

Casual conversations and occasional trade journal articles are seldom enough. Companies need to focus enough time on what they read, see, and hear about their markets to be able to spot critical changes in the economy, their markets, and their competition. They need to develop an ongoing system for monitoring customer attitudes, industry trends, technology changes, industry growth, and distribution changes.

Following is a selected list of simple and effective tactics that I have used over the years to gather market information. Each of these tactics can be accomplished on a tight budget and with limited staff and time.

1. *Use a clipping service.*   The same technique used to monitor competitors' activities can be used to understand what is going on in your markets. Have your secretary or a clipping service review industry trade journals and other marketing materials, and clip out the articles on customers, industry trends, technology changes, and other relevant matters, for you to read outside the office.

2. *Use your "office in the sky."*   Early in my career I found that time passed quickly if I had something to work on during long

airplane flights. Use your flying time to read all the marketing articles and do some of the marketing work that you can't do in the office. With a little organization and forethought, you can accomplish a tremendous amount during a coast-to-coast airplane flight.

3. *Make the library fun.* A lot of good business marketing information is available at the library. Major city, county, and university libraries now store an enormous amount of marketing articles on CD-ROM disks. If you can stop thinking of the library as the place to which you were sentenced to research boring college term papers, and instead learn to view your visits as part of the marketing game, they will become easy and entertaining.

4. *Do test marketing.* Testing products at the customer's plant is a terrific way to gather market and customer information. This approach can be as sophisticated as a beta test, a formal and often contractual way of testing your product in actual operation by allowing a customer to use it and report back strengths and weaknesses on a formal questionnaire, or as simple as letting prospects and customers play with demonstrator products. The point is to find out what people actually do with the products, and especially how the products help them to solve specific problems.

   Examples vary from sending prospects sample diskettes that demonstrate a new software program to installing expensive production machines on customers' production lines on a consignment basis. If you develop a good method for carefully recording the results, you will gain excellent customer and market data. If you gather results from a variety of customers, you'll gain a good feel for how the market as a whole will react to your products.

5. *Make systematic observations.* Everyone in the company observes customer or competitor behavior. The difference between casual observation and systematic observation is specifying (in writing) what you are looking for. For instance, most attendees at a trade show observe the competition, but nothing usually comes of it. Arm your trade show attendees with specific questions to ask, about matters such as why a prospect would or would not buy your product. Comparing the observations of several employees will provide you with some excellent market information.

6. *Measure what works.* SMMs gather a lot of data on their markets and customers every day, but they don't use it. The problem is that they have no useful way to turn data into strategy. For instance, direct mail and advertising inquiries may not be traced to sales, lost orders may not be followed up, warranty cards may get

lost in a file, service problems may not be tabulated, quotations may not be summarized, and sales trends may not be documented. Performing these simple clerical tasks can produce immediate information about customers and markets, for a relatively low cost. An efficient secretary or sales trainee, not a market research analyst, is all that is needed.

7. *Hire college students.* Use students to gather market information as well as competitor data. Some universities and especially business schools are looking for real-life topics for term projects. Students may even volunteer the time to do a market intelligence project for you.

8. *Examine your customers' visitors' books.* Always review the visitor's book in the lobby of every customer you visit to find out which competitors call on the account, and how often. If you have time, read it back as far as it goes. Be prepared to write down the names of the competitor's salespeople and the names of the buyers or specifiers they are calling on. Field salespeople routinely do this for their own benefit, but they rarely pass along the information. It's a good idea for owners and managers to check out visitors' books from time to time to keep them aware of competitors' activity.

9. *Take industry gurus to lunch.* Industry gurus, who are a great source of competitive information, can also provide you with information about market and industry trends. A guru may be a supplier, a consultant, an editor, a customer, a rep, or an association secretary. Use third parties and networking techniques to find out who the gurus are. Then make it a habit to ask them to lunch—and make sure you keep a dictaphone handy.

10. *Call a good customer.* Good customers are the hub of the market information wheel. Not only can they tell you about their wants and needs, and what competitors are up to; they can also suggest good agents and distributors, and they can give you their impressions of market and industry trends. Sometimes they are also industry gurus and thus are worth personal interviews.

11. *Take a competitor to lunch.* It's a good idea to take your competitors to lunch every now and then to discuss mutually interesting subjects about the industry, and to solicit their ideas about trends. Remember: you will never know what they can or will tell you unless you ask.

12. *Use sales calls to gather market information.* Sales calls also represent opportunities to find out things about your market and

customers. The trick is to quit selling for a moment, and to focus on listening and interviewing. Asking nonselling questions helps to build a customer relationship and can be a powerful market analysis tool.

*   *   *   *   *

Now that you have learned the basics of competitive and market intelligence, the next steps in business marketing are to define your market niches and to develop strategies for reaching them. These steps are the subject of Chapter 5.

KEY POINT

Given enough time, staff, and money, there is probably no limit to how much information you can gather on competitors and markets. Since few small manufacturers have these resources in unlimited quantities, it is important to identify the most important factors you need to investigate, and to begin a competitive and market intelligence program that fits your budget. The key is to make a commitment to gathering important information on a regular basis.

SUGGESTED ACTION

Call a meeting of key employees (including senior managers) to discuss ways of collecting competitive and market information on a regular basis, using some of the sources outlined in this chapter. Assign someone the task of collecting this information. Set aside an afternoon each month when all key employees will meet to review the new information collected and to discuss how it can be used to improve the competitive position of your company.

Chapter Five

Niche Marketing
Zeroing In on the Right Customers and Markets

There are hundreds and in some cases thousands of customers to choose from in any given industry. Different customers have different needs, and it is almost impossible for a small or midsize manufacturer to satisfy all of them. Some manufacturers spend enormous amounts of time, money, and energy on developing new products, and yet they never seem to find enough customers (or enough profitable customers) to justify the effort. The reason is that too many SMMs never bother to focus their efforts on finding the right market niches (customer groups) for their products.

Take the case of NeXT Systems, Inc., started by Apple Computer, Inc., cofounder Steven Jobs in 1987. You would think that with his proven entrepreneurial skills and his extraordinary experience of giving birth to the personal computer (PC) industry, Jobs would understand the computer market as well as anyone possibly could.

Ross Perot and Canon Ltd. believed he did. They added investment money to his capital, bringing the total seed money for Next Systems to $200 million. Jobs used the money to build an impressive new black magnesium computer, a "scholar's workstation," in Jobs's words. The product, targeted to the higher-education market, was priced at $10,000.

When the machine was unveiled, there was no rush to buy the high-ticket item, so NeXT Systems forged a partnership with the Businessland retail chain and attempted to sell the machines to the corporate market. In this market too, there were few takers, and Businessland eventually went into bankruptcy. Jobs and his partners decided to compete with Sun Microsystems in the workstation market, and they were moderately successful. The NeXT Systems computer, however, was not as powerful as some of the stronger competitors in this market and never reached its hoped-for potential. In mid-1993, Next sold its hardware business to Canon. Jobs had decided to switch to a software business and to try to compete with MicroSoft and Apple/IBM. Time will tell what becomes of this latest effort to find customers for its product.

NeXT Systems' workstation experiment is a classic example of a failure that occurred because the manufacturer never defined its market niche. The company produced a unique product with progressive features but didn't have a clear and accurate idea of who might use the product. As its name implied, the company always seemed to be concerned with the next step, the next model, and the next alliance. The company had plenty of talent and money behind it, but too much time was spent in developing the product and too little in analyzing the market.

ASK Computer Systems is a different story. ASK focused on its customers right from the beginning. Instead of building a product and then looking for buyers, the company carefully defined its customer base early in the development process.

In 1972, Sandra Kurtzig left her job with General Electric. Working out of her home and funded solely by her own $2,000 investment, Kurtzig set out to design specialized production software to help small manufacturers improve their manufacturing efficiency. At that time, manufacturing software was designed for large companies; no one was meeting the special needs of SMMs.

Kurtzig's new software package focused on controlling inventories and on coordinating engineering, purchasing, and production into an integrated system. Her program was designed to help SMMs reduce costs and was most applicable in small, fast-growing companies in which control problems increase exponentially with sales success.

Kurtzig was lucky enough (or smart enough) to design the program on a Hewlett-Packard (HP) computer. HP saw the program as an opportunity to sell more computers and agreed to distribute her product. ASK Computer Systems grew rapidly. Within 10 years, the company achieved $66 million in sales, and subsequently it grew to over $400 million in annual revenues.[1]

Sandra Kurtzig was successful for a number of reasons, but the primary reason was that she was an excellent niche marketer. She did not try to sell her product to all manufacturers. Instead, she focused her efforts on the needs of a well-defined market niche.

"ENTREPRENEURS CALL IT COMMON SENSE"

ASK Computer Systems is one of many business marketing success stories featured in *The Winning Performance*, by Donald K. Clifford, Jr., and Richard E. Cavanaugh. The book reports the results of the authors' study of 6,117 small manufacturing and service businesses in the United States that grew into successful midsize companies. The companies profiled in the book grew 4 times faster than Fortune 250 companies and 3.5 times faster than other, less successful midsize firms during the five-year period from 1978 to 1983.

The secret behind these success stories is that 90 percent of the companies chose to compete in small, well-defined market niches. Two-thirds of the companies generated half their annual revenues from market niches that they dominated.[2] The authors concluded:

> Midsize high growth companies succeed by identifying and meeting the needs of certain kinds of customers, not all customers, for special kinds of products and services, not all products and services. Business academics call this market segmentation. Entrepreneurs call it common sense.[3]

You should pursue a niche marketing strategy for the following six reasons:

1. *Efficiency.* You can reap more profit with fewer customers. SMMs often do not have the resources to penetrate large markets or to satisfy large numbers of customers. Focusing your resources on 150 targeted customers may be more profitable than selling to 1,500 shotgunned customers.

2. *Effectiveness.* Business-to-business customers buy solutions, not products. It is more effective to design products and services to solve the problems of a specific customer group than to try to suit a variety of different customers.

3. *Limited resources.* SMMs have limited money to spend on advertising, selling, and product development. Niche marketing strategies focus limited resources on specific customers in a carefully aimed "rifle-shot" approach to get the best bang for their buck.

4. *Competitive advantage.* Since their products and services are specifically designed to meet the needs of targeted customers better than the competition can, niche marketers gain competitive advantage.

5. *Customer retention and profits.* The point was made in Chapter 1 that repeat customers are more profitable than other customers. A

niche marketing strategy is the best way to ensure repeat business, because it emphasizes not only finding the right customers but retaining them.

6. *Quality.* Though every manufacturer in the country is in a sweat about improving quality, surprisingly few see the connection between quality and niche marketing. The truth is, it's a lot easier to improve quality when a company focuses its efforts on the needs of a few carefully targeted customers.

ASK Computer Systems and other high-growth technology companies have mastered niche marketing, but what about the average SMM? The answer is that any company can become an effective niche marketer, no matter what type of product it sells or how limited its resources. In fact, the more limited the resources of an SMM, the greater its need to pursue niche marketing.

Before we go any further, let's define a few terms. *Market segmentation* involves dividing a large market or customer list into niches—groups of customers with similar needs. *Target marketing* (also called *niche marketing*) is simply the strategies used to reach the niches.

Most books and articles about niche marketing make it sound difficult, but niche marketing doesn't need to be complicated to be effective. It might be as simple as having a sales manager review an account list in order to help the sales rep focus face-to-face selling time on customers with the greatest potential to buy.

For very small manufacturing companies, a niche might consist of just two or three large customers. The key to succeeding in niche marketing for SMMs is, "Keep it simple" (KIS).

Donald Hambrick, a professor at the Graduate School of Business at Columbia University in New York City, applauds the KIS approach to niche marketing. He has been quoted in *Business Marketing* as follows:

> I don't see market segmentation as being a function of analytic sophistication. It is just a matter of insight, instinct, and judgment. It's very much a mind-set of evaluating different customer types and needs. A good portion of it is frequently intuitive.[4]

A good deal of niche marketing is based on common sense. The technique involves constantly profiling customers; looking for common traits and needs; and tailoring products, services, and promotion to reach a specific group of customers. Many small manufacturers who are successful niche marketers seem to do it by intuition. Many SMMs realize they have to become niche marketers in order to survive. Some have become niche marketers because they recognized that they could not dominate large markets. They shrewdly decided to concentrate on a group of customers that they could protect and serve.

There are many ways to define market niches. Many SMMs simply define their customers by SIC codes, sales volume, company size, and/or geography. Even some large corporations, such as Unisys Corp. and Moore Corp. Ltd. (a manufacturer of business forms) use commonsense methods to define their niches. Unisys segments its customers by the products they buy, and Moore groups them by size.

ACADEMIC VERSUS PRACTICAL APPROACHES

The academic approach to niche marketing suggests that customers in an industry can be analytically profiled in terms of demographics, personality, and even behavior variables. The idea is to find out everything you can about your prospects and customers, right down to their decision-making style and the middle name of their firstborn children. This information is then fed into a mainframe computer by using multivariate analysis and other statistical techniques. Market niches are defined and measured for sales potential. The key to this approach is that the marketer defines the niches, by analyzing the data and prospects *first,* and develops products and strategies *second.*

This approach may work in the consumer marketing arena, but I have yet to see it applied in the world of business marketing, even by highly successful niche marketers. Instead, the process of defining or finding a niche often *begins* with a trial-and-error examination of a large number of customers or markets and eventually *ends* with identification of a profitable niche or niches.

This is not the same as shotgun marketing. Rather, successful SMMs start out with a rough idea of who might be interested in buying. They gradually narrow their focus, systematically eliminating prospects who don't turn out to be viable customers and modifying their products and services along the way in response to prospects who do show potential.

In the rest of this chapter I'll examine six practical approaches to niche marketing that have been used by six small manufacturers. These real-life examples will show you how other successful SMMs went about finding their market niches and will prove that niche marketing does not have to be expensive or complicated to be highly effective.

The six niche marketing approaches I'll discuss are:

1. Eliminating customers that are unprofitable or cannot be adequately supported after the sale (Singletech Inc.).
2. Focusing on product applications (FLIR Systems).
3. Letting a market niche emerge from a product line extension (Columbia Machine Inc.).
4. Finding an emerging market niche for a leading-edge product (Sequent Computer Systems).
5. Finding a niche by developing a substitute for an existing product (Ajax Foundry, Inc.).
6. Using telemarketing techniques to segment a mailing list and zero in on a market niche (Parsons Pine Products Inc.).

Eliminating Unprofitable Customers: Singletech Inc.

Niche marketing is based on the simple assumption that it's not possible or profitable for a company to provide excellent products and service to every known or possible customer. Many SMMs start out as shotgun marketers and accumulate a wide variety of customers that cost too much to reach or satisfy. At some point, the business either proves to be unprofitable or becomes inundated with service and customer problems.

Take the case of a small high-technology company I'll call Singletech Inc., a manufacturer of specialized, single-board computers. The company began as a mail-order business, shotgunned the marketplace, and ended up with a list of more than 1,000 business customers. OEMs, value-added resellers (VARs), industrial plants, hospitals, research labs, and universities were only some of the niches the company served. The problem was that every niche had a different set of needs. In trying to meet the needs of these various customers, Singletech wasn't serving any of them very effectively.

The situation begged the obvious question: Why not focus the company's resources on customers and prospects that represented the best opportunity for competitive advantage and profitable, long-term relationships, and eliminate the rest? That's just what Singletech set out to do.

Singletech's approach was to first analyze its customer list and subdivide it into groups of customers with similar needs. Next, it determined which groups were big enough and profitable enough to justify developing unique products and services for them. The steps in the process are described below.

Step 1: Assemble a customer list.   Singletech drew up a list of all the businesses that had purchased its products since it opened its doors. The list included information about total sales, profitability, products purchased, and SIC codes (if they were easy to determine).

Step 2: Subdivide customer groups by products and applications.   Next, customers were divided into groups according to the types of products they purchased and according to product applications. The objective was to eliminate customers that were not profitable or that weren't worth the effort to support.

Step 3: Identify the MVCs.   At the same time, Singletech identified its most valuable customers, by sales and profits. This was a revealing step: of the company's more than 1,000 customers, just 31 customers accounted for 80 percent of the sales volume during the most recent year, and 26 of these customers were OEMs.

Step 4: Eliminate unprofitable or problematic customer groups.   Next came the actual process of elimination. Commercial accounts were easily eliminated, because the analysis showed that they never ordered again and the marketing costs to find them exceeded their gross profit contribution. Most VARs were eliminated, because it was too costly for Singletech to stock their products and support them on specialized applications.

Most industrial plant customers were also eliminated because they used the products for custom production applications and seldom purchased again.

Step 5: Select the top market niche(s) and tailor services to suit it.   OEMs were clearly the market niche with the most immediate and long-term potential. Since some of the OEMs were already buying large quantities and had standardized their products to conform to Singletech's components, it only made sense to begin by focusing on their specific needs.

A customer needs survey revealed that the OEM classification could be further subdivided, and that Singletech would have to redesign some products and totally reorganize its sales department to support this group of MVCs.

Step 6: Target market to prospects with a similar profile. The last step for Singletech was to focus its advertising and promotion programs on finding more OEMs with similar needs.

Focusing on Product Applications: FLIR Systems

Richard Sears is a scientist who started an engineering consulting firm, FLIR Systems, in the mid-1970s. Sears's idea was to use a forward-looking infrared (FLIR) product to identify and locate heat loss in buildings. At the time, tax credits were being offered for energy conservation, and Sears recognized that the market potential for a FLIR product would be great. Initially he had no intention of building the product himself; he wanted to negotiate a licensing agreement with an existing manufacturer to use the product in his consulting work.

Sears knew of only one company, a Swedish firm, that had a commercially available infrared product that could be used to locate heat loss in buildings. The product, was a primitive one, and used low-resolution Polaroid pictures to show the results. Sears wanted to find a higher-quality device.

After considerable research, Sears tracked down a high-quality FLIR product manufactured by Aeroneutronic Ford, Inc., in Newport Beach, California. The device had been developed to image defects in the Alaska pipeline, but it was also used in classified military operations. For this reason, the company was reluctant to lend Sears the demo unit he needed to show investors in order to get funding for his company.

After lengthy negotiations, the company agreed to allow Sears to use one unit as a demo. Sears realized how advanced and how secret the technology was when he met the courier at the airport. The courier had the device handcuffed to his arm.

Sears demonstrated the unit to several investors, and they were impressed. The possibilities for commercial applications seemed endless.

Since he was unable to negotiate a licensing agreement with Aeroneutronic Ford, Sears decided to design and manufacture his own product. After 18 months of experimentation, FLIR Systems launched its first product, the Model 100A, to identify and locate heat loss in buildings.

Much of Sears's initial business was in energy conservation, an area that was profitable until 1980, when the government cut off requirements for mandatory infrared inspections to gain energy tax credits. By that time, FLIR Systems had run out of money by experimenting with a variety of other applications, none of which seemed commercially viable. Sears needed to find a commercially viable market niche quickly, so that he could convince investors to put more money into the company.

FLIR technology was new to the commercial marketplace, but Sears recognized that it had great potential. After experimenting with many kinds of products and applications from fire detection to military night reconnaissance projects, Sears stumbled upon the most promising niche at an annual national trade show of the International Helicopter Association in Las Vegas. At the show, he spoke to a number of helicopter operation managers and pilots who showed a strong interest in using a FLIR product on their helicopters at night for search-and-rescue and law enforcement applications. As a result of his discussions with these industry insiders, Sears and his partners decided to design the FLIR device into a protected sphere that could be mounted on a helicopter. The steps they subsequently followed are highlighted in Figure 5–1 and described below.

1. After identifying helicopter owners as a viable source of business, Sears investigated many potential helicopter applications, including the monitoring of power lines, military reconnaissance, forest fire detection, night law enforcement applications, and search-and-rescue missions.
2. Next, the company developed a prototype that could be mounted in a sphere for testing and certification on a helicopter.
3. Before Sears could demonstrate the new product, he had to acquire an experimental certificate from the Federal Aviation Administration (FAA).
4. Sears then found a directory which listed helicopter operators in all countries of the world. The directory specified the type of helicopter each operator used, its primary applications, and the name of a contact person.
5. Using the directory, Sears conducted a market survey to develop a prospect list of all nonmilitary organizations that had the potential to conduct helicopter surveillance or reconnaissance operations at night. The survey was limited to nonmilitary organizations and was only one information gathering technique. The sales department also worked on other accounts, including military to identify orga-

FIGURE 5–1
FLIR Systems, Inc. (*Focusing on Product Applications*)

1. Identified helicopter operators as a market niche.
2. Designed a thermal imaging prototype.
3. Acquired an FAA certificate.
4. Found a global directory of helicopter operators.
5. Used the directory to conduct a market survey.
6. Built model 100A for demonstrations. Explored many applications including:
   • Military night reconnaissance.
   • Night surveillance.
   • Fire detection.
   • Law enforcement.
   • Search-and-rescue operations.
   • Agricultural croplands.
   • Location of defects in underground pipelines.
   • Border patrol.
   • The mapping of forest fires.
7. Focused on the best three niches:
   • Police departments—night vision for crime detection.
   • Governmental agencies—search-and-rescue applications.
   • Military—night surveillance.
8. Began a sales campaign.

nizations with the potential for making requests for quotations (RFQs).

6. Demo units of Model 100A were built and demonstrated to prospects, who were selected because of their short-term needs and/or their potential for RFQs. Factory people were involved in all demonstration projects so that they could get customer feedback and bring back product and applications data that would be useful in modifying the prototype. (I'll discuss this in more detail in Chapter 8.)

7. From the data gathered in the field, Sears decided to focus on the three subniches in the helicopter market that seemed to have the best sales potential:

   • Law enforcement departments, which could use FLIR devices to help combat crime.
   • The US Coast Guard, which needed FLIR devices for search-and-rescue missions.

- Military services, which could use FLIR devices in night surveillance.

8. The sales department began a systematic investigation of governmental agencies, military organizations, and law enforcement agencies, looking for contract and bid opportunities in these areas.

FLIR won its first big contract from the Coast Guard in 1983, after
competing with some major manufacturers of night vision devices. This
order provided evidence to the investors that a large search-and-rescue
market niche existed and that FLIR Systems was very competitive. The
investors subsequently made a major infusion of capital into the firm, providing enough growth to permit FLIR to fund the development of additional products.

The FLIR Systems story demonstrates that considerable experimentation is usually required to find the right market niche for a product. First,
the company had to determine the most viable overall market, which
turned out to be helicopter operators. Once this customer base was identified, it was relatively easy to find out which niches held the most potential.

Even though a trial-and-error process was used in FLIR System's
marketing approach, this was by no means a shotgun program. The
company used a systematic, step-by-step approach to selection and definition of its niche.

Thanks to its efforts in narrowing down the possibilities and finding a
high-potential market niche, FLIR grew from a small research company
with $250,000 in sales in 1980 to a publicly held, midsize firm with rev-
enues of $38 million in 1993. The company's infrared night vision sys-
tems are used all over the world by private companies, foreign
governments, and military organizations.

Profiling the End User: Columbia Machine

In the late 1960s, when the market for copying machines and copy paper
was growing by leaps and bounds, Xerox Corporation wrote a specification to its suppliers on how to handle paper cases and loads to reduce
paper damage. This specification caused paper mills to rethink their warehouse systems and to look for new methods and equipment to handle the
cartons of copy paper.

The company I worked for at the time, Columbia Machine Inc., manufactured palletizers—large, custom-built machines that automatically

stack cartons into pallet loads from a conveyor line. We were asked to bid on manufacturing a machine with the equipment to meet the new specification from Xerox.

We modified a standard design and added a new "turntable" device that would gently turn the Xerox cases in either direction without touching the sides of the cases. This simple line extension gave us a unique competitive advantage, and we received an order for nine machines from a large paper company.

In the mid-1970s, I had the opportunity to work with an engineer at Nekoosa Paper Company, one of our customers, to refine this turntable-type machine to connect to a new high-speed sheeter manufactured by E.C.H. Will of Hamburg, Germany. A sheeter is a huge production machine that converts large rolls of paper into sheets of photocopy paper. Will's new sheeter could run three times faster than equivalent American machines.

Nekoosa's machine was the second of these new German sheeters installed in the United States. Everyone in the paper industry was waiting to see how the new German machines would impact the marketplace. Even though the machines were more expensive than their American counterparts, they were supposed to increase productivity enough to pay for the investment in a few years. I knew that if this proved to be true, there would be opportunities for the new sheeters in many US paper companies with converting operations, and Columbia Machine wanted to be there first.

We built several of our modified palletizers for Nekoosa, and they worked very well. I decided to do a little research and define this emerging market niche more clearly. I started by analyzing the profile of our customer, Nekoosa. Here's what I found:

1. Nekoosa was a large, multiplant paper company with converting lines.
2. The company had several of the original, low-speed Lenox (American-manufactured) sheeters.
3. Nekoosa was interested in the new German sheeter because it provided higher speeds, less downtime, and more precision, and boosted the overall level of production.

In researching further, I found that the copy paper segment of the paper industry was growing 10 to 15 percent a year and that many large paper companies had special converting lines and contracts to make copy paper. From several paper industry associations we got lists of all paper and pulp mills in the United States. The total was fewer than 200 companies, so it was a simple matter to find other mills with the same profile as Nekoosa.

E.C.H. Will had already done a good job of examining the US market and had targeted many paper mills as candidates for new lines in the United States. I had a good contact at Will, so I knew which mills were being targeted. We also found, by visiting the mills, that every manager and specifier in them was a member of TAPPI (Technical Association of Pulp and Paper Industry), the major paper industry trade association. These members gave us enough in-depth knowledge of the customer's needs to refine the machine even further and build overwhelming competitive advantage.

From the beginning, we were determined to dominate this market niche and to stay ahead of our competitors, and we devoted part of our advertising budget to buying targeted ads in a paper industry trade journal. In addition to offering a heavy-duty, customized machine, we offered many special services to these targeted customers. As a result of our efforts, we won a number of new long-term customers, and the modified palletizer had the highest gross margin of any of the machines in the product line.

This niche strategy worked well for both E.C.H. Will and Columbia Machine. Between 1975 and 1984, 100 Will sheeters were installed in the United States, and Columbia Machine received 99 of the palletizer orders for these new lines. Our sole competitor, who refused to acknowledge the impact of the German machine on the US market, got only one of the new orders.

Finding an Emerging Niche for a Leading-Edge Product: Sequent Computer Systems

Perhaps the most difficult marketing problem of all is to identify a niche for a breakthrough product in an emerging market. That's what Sequent Computer was faced with in the early 1980s.

Sequent Computer, a small start-up company, had been founded in 1983 by a group of ex-employees of Intel to build parallel processing computers. (Parallel processing is a method of linking multiple processors to perform complex tasks much faster than a single computer could.) Collectively the founders had more than 50 years of marketing experience in similar technology industries.

The strategy for Sequent was to buy commercially available microprocessors and other components and to avoid the long start-up period involved in inventing brand-new technology. In searching for a market niche, the company's original strategy was to search for "early adopters" of the new parallel processing technology—the buyers who would be willing to take a chance on new products before most others were ready to buy.

Sequent began its search by calling on OEMs that produced computer-aided design (CAD), computer-aided manufacturing (CAM), and computer-aided engineering (CAE) software; automatic test equipment; military computer applications; robotics; simulation applications; and artificial intelligence. Sequent founders also called on university research labs and weapons labs. The buyers in most of these market niches were engineers and scientists. By attending trade shows, making field sales calls, studying a few published market research reports, and doing a tremendous amount of phone work, the founders were able to try out their new technology idea on a wide variety of technical buyers.

Because there was a lot of interest in parallel processing, the founders were able to test the viability of their product concept, even though they hadn't yet built a demonstration unit. The company never used quantitative market research techniques in trying to find a niche. Instead, its founders relied on qualitative techniques to identify key industry people, companies that were trend setters, and customers with a need for high-speed number crunching.

On the basis of the information generated during the research stage, the founders decided to appoint task forces and hire specialists to examine some targeted customers and applications, from medical imaging to molecular modeling, in more detail.

Because their new computers would require sophisticated software, the founders decided to approach some of the emerging database companies, such as Oracle and Relational Technologies, as potential partners who could test the validity of their product ideas. Ultimately, Sequent Computers signed a joint agreement with Oracle to develop a parallel processing system.

After many field sales calls and high-level visits with corporate executives, the founders began to eliminate companies and market niches that didn't seem to offer an adequate payback. The OEM and technical markets did have applications for the product and provided enough sales to "kick start" the company. But, in the long term, the commercial applications seemed to have more potential and provided important early sales.

From their market investigation, the founders knew that users that had to manipulate huge amounts of data at high speeds might be able to justify the cost of a system because it would enable them to handle data faster. Sequent began to focus its efforts on companies that used mainframe computers to handle high-speed commercial transactions.

At the same time that market development work was going on in the United States, Sequent Computer was carrying on discussions with the giant German technology company, Siemens. Siemens had been trying to develop a parallel processing technology of its own, but had been beaten to the marketplace by a competitor. Siemens, which was also selling to high-speed transaction processing end users, decided to buy a parallel processing computer system from Sequent rather than spending the time and money to develop one of its own. Siemens became a reseller for Sequent and represented its first entree into the European market. Once Sequent had finally found its niche, it began focusing its product development and marketing efforts. Sales took off in 1985. By 1992 Sequent had grown to become a $200 million company with more than 1,000 employees.

I asked Larry Wade (who has moved on to pursue other interests) what he had learned from his experience with Sequent Computers that could be applied to other small manufacturers. He offered the following advice: "In the early stages of any start-up company, beggars can't be choosers. A company needs sales from almost anywhere, and it is valid to sell to many markets just to analyze the opportunities. "But at some point in time you've got to focus on a group of customers. Companies who never really find their focus in the market never find profitability."

Creating a Substitute Product for an Existing Niche: Ajax Foundry

Another way to expand a business is by developing a substitute product for an existing market niche. In the case of a small company I'll call Ajax Foundry, Inc., the substitute product was an expendable wear part on a machine.

In 1973, a consultant to the paper industry brought the company a casting called a *refiner plate,* which was used as a wear part in a larger machine called a *refiner.* Refiners are used in pulp and paper processing to prepare wood chips and pulp stock for use in paper manufacturing.

The consultant had gotten the plate from a local paper mill that was interested in finding another supplier of the wear part, because the OEM was high-priced and unresponsive. This case offers a classic example of a large OEM focusing on the overall product but not paying attention to the small wear parts that go in it. Such oversights present excellent opportunities for SMMs to develop substitute products and find ready-made market niches.

In essence, Ajax Foundry was asked to copy the part and start supplying it to the local mill. The process Ajax used to find and develop the refiner plate market niche had five phases, which are described below.

Phase 1: The alliance stage. First, Ajax forged an alliance with the dissatisfied local paper mill. After considerable trial and error, and with the support of the paper mill's engineers, Ajax produced a refiner plate that could replace the existing part and sell for about 25 percent less.

Phase 2: Looking for opportunities. After this initial success, the owners of Ajax Foundry decided to approach other mills in the Northwest and offer to copy their refiner plates as well. Many mills had different kinds of refiners, which would require manufacture of castings to custom specifications, but once Ajax developed the custom plates for the machines, a steady flow of repeat business could be anticipated. Since Ajax had a 25 percent price advantage over the only two competitors in the industry, paper mills gradually took notice and sales began to improve.

Phase 3: The technology stage. After a year or two of experimenting with different plates, Ajax decided to form an engineering department, in order to develop the technology further. The company hired an engineer away from a competitor and began improving the refiner plate designs, on the basis of its employees' experience and ideas. At this point, Ajax was no longer making copies of other manufacturers' refiner plates. Instead, they were developing new plate designs that were more durable and less expensive.

Phase 4: The target marketing stage. Ajax joined a paper industry association, which put the company in touch with most of the people in US paper mills who were concerned with refiners. In the association's directory, Ajax identified a number of mills that used refiner plates. The company's subsequent marketing efforts were targeted at these prospects.

Ajax factory salespeople began to contact each mill to find out prospective customers' specific needs. The strategy was to offer the mills lower-cost, custom-designed refiner plates and fast, personal service.

During this phase, Ajax got a boost from two large refiner competitors that decided to merge and consolidate their manufacturing facilities. The consolidation was a disaster for the competitors but a boon to Ajax, which increased its market share while the merged companies struggled to work out their manufacturing problems. Within two years of the consolidation, Ajax tripled its revenues, growing from $2 million to $6 million, and became recognized as one of the leading suppliers in its market niche.

Phase 5: Product line extension.   After succeeding in the refiner plate market niche, the company's next step was to look for other parts in the refiner machine system that Ajax might redesign in order to create another market niche opportunity. The company focused on a part called the *plug feeder,* which was being manufactured in Europe and shipped to the United States. Ajax knew that it would have a cost advantage if it could produce the product at home. In addition, the company's engineers had some ideas on how to improve the existing technology, which would make the new product even more competitive.

The strategy succeeded. The second niche product gained immediate recognition, since Ajax knew all the customers in the niche and had already established a good reputation.

One of the primary reasons for Ajax Foundry's success was that the owners were market-driven people who were willing to take risks and perhaps even lose a little money for a couple of years in order to gain acceptance in a new market niche. The company also had the sense not to compete on the entire product, which would have been extremely expensive, but to focus on an area of weakness, in which it could gain a competitive advantage. Finally, Ajax didn't develop a second product until it had made certain that the first one was a success and had firmly established itself in the market niche.

Mailing List Segmentation: Parsons Pine Products

Parsons Pine Products Inc. is a company that has always understood value-added products and niche markets. It was founded in 1947 on the idea of making products out of trim ends (a waste lumber product) and Jim Parsons spent years developing a fine-cutting saw technology that could cut so thin and smooth that it reduced waste by producing more parts and less sawdust. This technology allowed the company to develop value-added products, from wooden rulers to mousetrap blanks, for a variety of market niches.

In 1989, Jerry Sivin took over the operations of the company and became a partner in the business. He immediately set out to find ways to grow the business. One of the company's biggest products was wooden door louvers. This niche was profitable, but it was a seasonal business that slowed down in the wintertime.

Sivin knew he needed to find other market niches that could fill the seasonal gap. He felt there might be opportunities in the toy market. For one thing, the toy industry used many small wooden parts, and Parsons was highly automated and well equipped to do high-volume, small parts production. Sivin also knew that the toy market demanded product in the last half of the year, which coincided with the slack time in Parson's other major product line.

Sivin knew that toy manufacturers had to buy their material through brokers at less than truckload quantities. He knew that negotiating direct contracts with mills could give Parsons a price advantage. He also knew that the fine-cut saw technology would allow him to get more out of each piece of wood, and that he could use wood that was considered waste in the Northwest. Furthermore, Parsons was expert at designing and modifying its own automation machinery and might be able to custom-design some equipment that could improve production and lower costs.

No one in the company was familiar with the toy industry, so Jerry Sivin decided to take a methodical approach to exploring this new market niche opportunity. Here are the steps he took:

1. *Mailing list.* Parsons purchased a mailing list of toy manufacturers that listed them by volume sold, number of employees, material used, and the manufacturing reps they used.

2. *Segmentation.* The company examined all the toy companies on the list and picked out manufacturers by product type (companies that marketed wooden toys) and by total sales (companies with a minimum of $1 million in annual revenues).

3. *Target market.* From this segmented list, Parsons selected about 300 companies for a telemarketing program. A sales pitch was developed, which explained the advantages of doing business with Parsons and showed how cost and technical advantages could lead to lower costs for customers. At the end of the pitch, the

telemarketer asked if Parsons could get product specifications and send a formal proposal to the company.

4. *Results.*   The telemarketing effort paid off. Parsons reached 150 companies, sent out 24 proposals, and received three contracts to manufacture Lincoln Logs, play blocks, and parts for scientific toy sets. The Lincoln Logs contract was secured after Parsons agreed to develop a new machine, partially funded by the customer, to produce the logs.

The toy market niche was so successful that Parsons sold all the capacity of its plant the second year and provided steady employment for 110 employees. Under Jerry Sivin's guidance, Parsons grew from $3.5 million to $7.5 million in sales within three years.

Jerry Sivin suggests that any small manufacturer who wants to explore niche markets (especially in the wood products industry) should:

- Develop a "100 percent customer orientation" or they won't survive.
- Keep the project simple and use a pragmatic approach. It takes good common sense and lots of hours, not fancy marketing techniques, to be successful.
- Look at niche marketing as a partnership between the right manufacturer and the right customer.

As the stories above illustrate, the search for a market niche seldom begins with defining the right customers using a sophisticated computer model. In most cases, it's experimentation, through trial and error with many customers and many markets, that ultimately results in a defined niche.

The trial-and-error process is well worth the effort. The superiority of the niche marketing approach over shotgunning is summed up nicely by Lois Moore and Daniel Plung, who write:

> If a firm develops a marketing strategy that is uniquely suited to solving one group's problems, they will be more successful at solving that problem than the firm that tries to solve all of the problems of everyone. In trying to reach everyone, the firm successfully reaches no one.[5]

* * * * *

In this chapter you learned how to identify niche markets and customers. Now you can turn your attention to developing products and services tailored to their needs—the subject of Chapter 6.

KEY POINT

Successful niche marketers know how to focus their time and resources on the right customers—those who have similar needs. And they tailor their products and services so that they do a better job than their competitors of meeting these customers' needs.

SUGGESTED ACTION

Print out a list of all of your customers and try to group them into market niches by size, product, SIC code, or any other parameter suggested in this chapter. Can you profile customers in each niche well enough to develop a targeted mailing list of similar companies?

NOTES

1. Donald K Clifford, Jr., and Richard E Cavanaugh, *The Winning Performance* (New York: Bantam Books, 1986), pp. 55–58.
2. Ibid., p. 53.
3. Ibid., p. 6.
4. Quoted in Kate Bertrand, "Harvesting the Best," *Business Marketing,* October 1988, p. 41.
5. Lois K Moore and Daniel L Plung, *Marketing Technical Ideas and Products Successfully* (New York: Institute of Electrical and Electronics Engineers and Free Press, 1984), p. 94.

Chapter Six

Customer-Driven Product Development
A Proven Formula for New Product Success

In the Introduction, I noted that two MIT professors, Michael Piore and Charles Sable, were among the first to predict the move from mass marketing to customized, flexible production. This trend has led to a proliferation of new products and competitors, and has forced product development to become an integral part of the marketing effort of all small and midsize manufacturers who hope to succeed in the 1990s and beyond.

Much has been written about product development, but most of it has been written for and about large companies with significant resources. Product development is just as important for SMMs, as noted above. The difference is that SMMs have limited resources to devote to new product development and often don't have the reserves to recover from major new product failures. The purpose of this chapter is to increase the chances of your success in product development by helping you to involve your customers more in the process and by showing you the mistakes and successes of other SMMs.

THE PRODUCT RANGE

Before getting into the details of new product development, it's important to examine the wide range of products that manufacturers market to other businesses—from simple office products to nuclear power plants.

Figure 6–1 illustrates the vast range of business products. Many people believe that "marketing is marketing" and that the same principles and strategies apply to any product. This assumption is not true. The marketing strategies for industrial products and for consumer products are very different. Marketing strategies also vary greatly among the many categories of business and industrial products.

For example, the selling, promotion, and pricing strategies used to sell low-unit-price, standard motors to known accounts are fairly straightforward. The strategies needed to sell automatic machinery, which is large, complex, and expensive, and which is funded by capital project requests, are far more complicated and costly. In this chapter (and throughout this book), I am focusing primarily on the complex, expensive, customized products on the right-hand side of the product range shown in Figure 6–1.

WHY NEW PRODUCTS FAIL

New product development is a high-stakes game that can catapult a company into riches or plunge it into bankruptcy in a short period of time. Studies by The Conference Board and other research organizations show that approximately one-third of all new products introduced to the marketplace are failures. When all the new product concepts that never make it to the commercialization stage are included, the success rate is only one out of every seven new product ideas (Figure 6–2).

In an empirical study entitled "Why New Industrial Products Fail,"[1] Robert Cooper analyzed 150 industrial product firms, large and small, and discovered that most of the reasons for new product failures had to do with marketing rather than technical problems. Specifically, companies underestimated the number and strength of competitors, overestimated the number of potential users, and overestimated the price customers would pay for the product. Other studies have come to similar conclusions.

In my experience, SMMs tend to focus much of their money, effort, and time on the internal development process and few of these resources on studying customers and markets to find out what products they want. (This is not true of companies that have strong marketing champions on staff.) Cooper also cited this as a reason for failure. He pointed out that when there is an inward orientation, manufacturers tend to overestimate the number of potential users and the price they will pay for a new product. He concluded, "A greater market orientation is required as part of the new product development effort."

FIGURE 6–1

Product Range (*Variations in Business Products*)

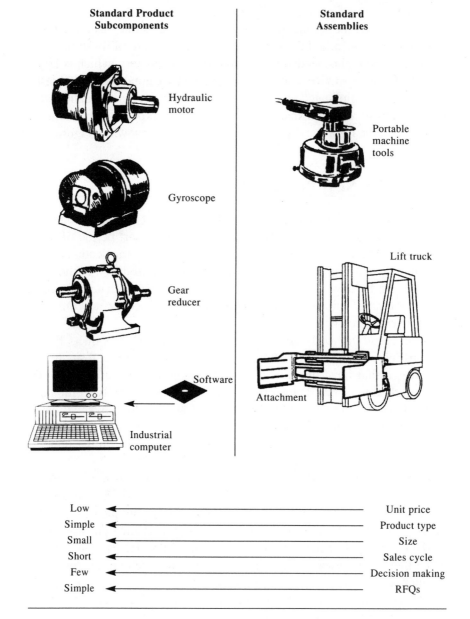

	Custom and Batch		Engineered Systems

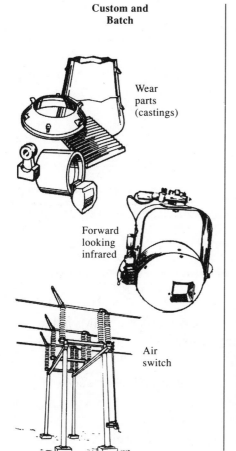

Wear
parts
(castings)

Forward
looking
infrared

Air
switch

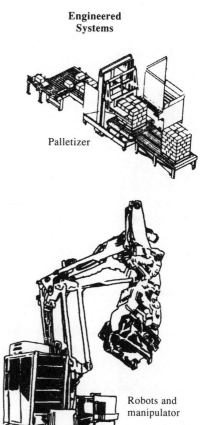

Palletizer

Robots and
manipulator

Unit price	────────────────────────▶	High
Product type	────────────────────────▶	Complex
Size	────────────────────────▶	Large
Sales cycle	────────────────────────▶	Long
Decision making	────────────────────────▶	Many
RFQs	────────────────────────▶	Complex

FIGURE 6–2
The Attrition Rate of New Products

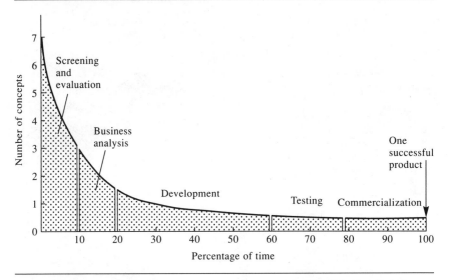

Source: Adapted with permission from *New Product Management for the 1980s* (New York: Booz Allen & Hamilton, 1982).

Many new products never make it to market because SMMs fail to undertake one or more of the following actions (all of them *externally* focused) that are vital to a successful product development effort:

1. Identification of market niches and a reasonable estimation of the number of potential users.
2. Profiling of customers to determine their needs.
3. Identification of all competitor companies and their strengths and weaknesses.
4. Identification of competitive or substitute products.
5. Development of a unique product idea, with input from customers.
6. Establishment of a competitive price.

I don't want to convey the impression that small manufacturers understand these six factors any less then their big brothers. In many cases, they do a better job than larger firms in developing new products. But product failure is more devastating to small companies, so it's more important for them to learn how to avoid it.

THE PITFALLS OF THE "NEW PRODUCT GAME"

The difference between success and failure lies in knowing how to avoid the common pitfalls of the *new product game*. Figure 6–3 illustrates some of the most obvious pitfalls that SMMs encounter in playing this high-stakes game. As exaggerated as the problems might appear in the figure, elements of these problems can be found in the product development process of most SMMs.

The game begins with the inventor, designer, or creator of the product idea (1). There is a tendency for the inventor to become so wrapped up in the product idea and to ignore customer needs. Without any input from other people in the company or the outside world, the inventor starts to believe that the product is unique, even if it's not (2).

Once engineers get involved, there is a tendency for them to play with the technology and to push performance for performance's sake (engineers love to tinker), rather than because this is what the customer wants (3).

So far, most of the SMM's resources have been focused on developing the product; little time or money has been spent on researching the market or customers. The company just assumes that there will be plenty of customers who are willing to buy the product (4).

Since no customers have been identified and no market niches defined, the advertising department must use a shotgun approach to generate interest in and inquiries about the product (5). At the same time, the sales manager must develop a sales forecast that will justify product development expenditures (6), even though no one has any idea of what to expect in terms of sales.

Because the product specifications are still undefined, the manufacturing department can't design an economical production process, and this results in initial manufacturing costs that are unnecessarily high (7). The prototype is built and tested without much customer input, and the product is moved into production (8).

The unfortunate salesperson is now stuck with the job of finding and selling a product to unknown customers, without any information on why anyone would buy the new product (9). Not surprisingly, most customers decide not to buy (10).

After the money has been spent and it becomes apparent that sales are not forthcoming, there is always a lot of frustration, anger, and finger pointing (usually the fingers are pointed at the sales force). The conversation between the president or owner of the SMM and the sales manager goes something like the dialogue below.

FIGURE 6–3
The New Product Game

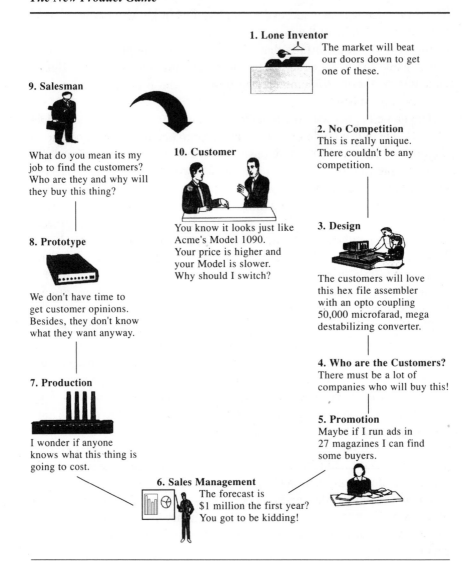

1. Lone Inventor
The market will beat
our doors down to get
one of these.

9. Salesman

What do you mean its my
job to find the customers?
Who are they and why will
they buy this thing?

10. Customer

2. No Competition
This is really unique.
There couldn't be any
competition.

8. Prototype

You know it looks just like
Acme's Model 1090.
Your price is higher and
your Model is slower.
Why should I switch?

3. Design

We don't have time to
get customer opinions.
Besides, they don't know
what they want anyway.

The customers will love
this hex file assembler
with an opto coupling
50,000 microfarad, mega
destabilizing converter.

4. Who are the Customers?
There must be a lot of
companies who will buy this!

7. Production

I wonder if anyone
knows what this thing is
going to cost.

5. Promotion
Maybe if I run ads in
27 magazines I can find
some buyers.

6. Sales Management
The forecast is
$1 million the first year?
You got to be kidding!

Source: The Harvard Graphics program is a product of Software Publishing Corporation and has no
connection with Harvard University.

Bill, the president, has just called Ron, the sales manager, into his office. Bill's face is beet-red, as he prepares to launch his attack on Ron:

Bill:

You know the company has invested a heck of a lot of money in the Model 8000 skridget. Joe [Bill's son-in-law, who manages engineering] spent an enormous amount of time perfecting the Model 8000, and we spent three months running it in the shop. Joe told me that there was only one other similar product in the United States, and that we would have a lock on the skridget market. We've spent a fortune trying to give you something else to sell, and now frankly, I don't think your reps are even interested.

Ron:

Customers are telling us the price is too high and that there are a lot of products like the Model 8000.

Bill:

[*grimacing and turning an even brighter shade of red*] "If I were you, Ron, I would find a way to get those salespeople off their butts. If you can't do it, I'll find someone who can.

The High Cost of Redesign

When a new product like the skridget bombs in the marketplace, salespeople have no choice but to find out why it doesn't meet the needs of customers. Customers usually offer suggestions for modification, and the changes have to be implemented during the selling phase of the process. The problem is that changes are very expensive at this stage.

Every time the new product moves to the next step in the process, the costs jump dramatically and the risk of failure increases proportionately. During the concept or idea stage, changes in the product are relatively inexpensive, but they accelerate exponentially as the product nears production.

Making changes after a product has been introduced to the market is a problem, because by this time the SMM may have run out of funds to continue development or to support the field problems. Also, since so much money has already been invested, management tends to resist spending more to make modifications, and the problems are automatically transferred to the sales department once more.

THE IMPORTANCE OF CUSTOMER-DRIVEN PRODUCT DEVELOPMENT

By now, you can begin to understand why talking to customers from the early stages of the process is so crucial to the success of any product development effort. The following true story will demonstrate the rewards of asking customers what they want rather than imposing unwanted products on them.

In 1981, Gerry Langeler and his partners left the electronics giant Tektronix to start a new company. Their plan was to develop a new software product for the emerging computer-aided engineering (CAE) market. Langeler's new enterprise, like most start-up companies, had limited funding, and the partners had to work out of their homes to develop their new product idea. They named the new company Mentor Graphics.

After spending weeks developing the specifications for the new product, the partners had progressed to a point at which they were convinced that their invention could revolutionize the CAE market. Unlike the founders of many high-technology start-ups, Langeler and his partners knew they had to get a reaction from the marketplace before they asked people to invest the large sums of money that would be needed to launch the product. They chose 20 companies in the United States that they considered potential customers in this emerging market niche, and discussed their product idea with these companies.

The target companies not only told Langeler and his partners about their needs and problems but also helped in the process of changing the specifications to meet their future needs. After a whirlwind customer trip, lasting four weeks, the partners returned home with a completely revised software product and several potential customers. There was still a lot of work to be done, but the founders of Mentor Graphics had defined customer needs well enough to design a leading-edge product that achieved phenomenal success. In its first year of business, this customer-driven company achieved revenues of $1.7 million. Within eight years, it had grown to $400 million in sales. In the early 1990s Mentor Graphics continued to lead the industry in revenues and in new product development.

In a presentation I attended in 1990, Gerry Langeler, president and chief operating officer (COO) of Mentor Graphics, spoke about the lessons he learned during the process of starting up the company. I believe these lessons apply to every small manufacturer:

1. Let the market determine the specifications for your product. Use potential customers as collaborators in the design process.

2. You have more competition than you think. None of Mentor Graphics's most important competitors were even identified in the original business plan.

3. Talk to potential customers during the design phase. For the founders of Mentor Graphics, seeing potential customers face-to-face was an essential step in refining the new product idea and establishing market potential.

I'll discuss each of these items in more detail later in this chapter, when I present the 10-step process for achieving new product success.

THE THREE BASIC PRODUCT TYPES

A manufacturer that wants to develop a new product must first decide what type of product to make. The choice of product will depend in large part on the company's resources. Products differ greatly in terms of risk, cost, marketing and promotional strategies, and commitment required to develop them. Obviously, it is more costly to develop a brand-new technology than to modify an existing product. Choosing a new product that fits the company budget is an important decision.

New products can be divided into three categories:

- Product modifications or line extensions.
- Replacement and substitute products.
- Leading-edge products.

Let's take a closer look at each product type.

Product Modifications or Line Extensions

Included in this category are redesigns of existing products to reduce manufacturing costs, products that are given new features, and new models that are introduced to expand the product line. The commitment and risks involved in developing these products are relatively low, and the strategy is usually to sell the new products to the same customers and markets.

It's important to get customers' input about product modifications and line extensions, even though they are only variations on current products. The example of PASCOR Inc. will show why.

PASCOR is a small manufacturer of high-voltage air switches for utility substation and transmission lines. Utilities don't always have the luxury of building new transmission lines, because of environmental pressures. Instead, they must find ways to transmit more power over existing lines. To do so, they need heavy-duty components that are easily replaceable.

PASCOR saw this market opportunity and began looking for new product opportunities for its line of air switches. According to Kathy Wakefield, marketing manager, the way to find new product ideas was obvious. "You listen to customer complaints and service suggestions. We found that if you have a systematic way of documenting customer comments, many new product ideas will present themselves. All of our products have to be ANSI [American National Standards Institute] tested, which costs us $50 to $100,000 per product; and we cannot afford to test a product no one will buy."

PASCOR spends the time necessary for gathering customer data, and then engineers a prototype. The new product is developed into a working prototype and is mounted on a trailer to demonstrate the idea at the customer's plant. This method gives customers the opportunity to see and feel the concept, and it gives PASCOR a perfect method for gathering the final data necessary to finalize the product for tests and certification. "Our system to develop new products works very well," said Wakefield, "because the end users have a hand in the development and it paves the way to immediate sales."

Replacement and Substitute Products

Some products may be new to the manufacturer but similar to other products in the market. I refer to these as *replacement products.* For instance, an electronic components manufacturer might develop a data-acquisition device for monitoring production machines. The product might be a first for the company, but there are hundreds of similar devices on the market.

Then there are products that are very different from anything on the market, but that do the same job as other products on the market. These are generally referred to as *substitute products.* For example, pneumatic guns can be substituted for hammers, plastic parts are a substitute for steel parts, adhesives can be used instead of fasteners, and plated screws can take the place of deck nails.

Small manufacturers often make the mistake of believing that a product such as a hammer is not a direct competitor for a product like an adhesive. They completely overlook the substitute as a customer alternative when they are developing new products.

Leading-Edge Products

Leading-edge products are both new to the manufacturer and unique in the marketplace. Leading-edge products are very risky and have a high failure rate. On the positive side, when they are successful the returns are truly spectacular and can lead to the creation of whole new markets.

Most leading-edge products that are expensive new technologies requiring many years to commercialize are developed by large corporations. Microprocessors, carbon fiber plastics, and new drugs are three examples.

The leading-edge products of small manufacturers are generally adaptive or innovative products based on these new technologies. For example, development of the microprocessor led to the development of thousands of microprocessor-based new products by small companies.

DECIDING WHICH PRODUCT TYPE TO DEVELOP

As noted above, new product categories involve different levels of risk and commitment. Understanding the choices will help the small manufacturer to choose the approach that will best fit the resources of the company. The challenge involves, first, balancing the risk involved against the resources available and, second, making sure that you will be able to support the new product before you proceed to the development phase.

The most obvious choice for SMMs who can't afford the risk of expensive failures is to develop product modifications. The customers are already known and have experience with the products, and the investment is usually modest and low-risk. Perhaps the best policy is to make sure that you have explored all opportunities with current customers before running off into the uncharted and possibly stormy waters of leading edge products and new markets.

With substitute and leading edge products, the investment is higher and the risks are much greater. As noted above, the opportunities are also greater because the company can expand into new markets and generate additional revenues.

The greatest danger for substitute or replacement products is that they will become "me-too" products that don't offer unique benefits.

The me-too problem is one of the biggest reasons why sales do not materialize for many new products. The only solution is to invest the time to find competitors and their products early in the process.

The Man Who Walked on Water

Ralph Shaw, of Shaw Venture Partners in Portland, Oregon, knows the ups and downs of new product development and start-up companies better than most people do. For 30 years, Shaw has been evaluating and investing in small and large businesses. He reads 400 to 500 business plans a year. As a director of more than 10 private firms and the portfolio manager of several highly successful investment companies, he has enough experience to know the problems involved in new product development. He told me a story about a unique invention that illustrates the problems of me-too products.

After Shaw got started as a venture capitalist in Portland, Oregon, a man called him up and said he had a unique invention that would enable him to walk on Tillamook Bay (on the Oregon coast). Shaw said, "You mean you can walk on water?" The man replied that he had invented a retractable walking device that could be strapped to the legs and that would enable a person to walk on the mud of Tillamook Bay while the tide was out.

Ralph Shaw thought this invention had to be the only one of its kind in the world. He decided that it was worth evaluating, and spent a lot of time looking for market niches and applications. This was in the early 1980s, and Shaw thought the device might have a military application in the Iran-Iraq war, in which hundreds of soldiers were being trapped and killed in shallow water.

His partners thought he was crazy, but he continued to work with the inventor, trying to find a market and funding for the project. After considerable research, his company decided not to fund the project because the start-up costs and development risks were too high.

Soon afterward, Shaw found in the local newspaper a picture of what appeared to be the same invention. He followed up and found that another man had independently invented the same product in Minnesota. According to Ralph Shaw, the moral of the story is, "There are very few really unique products in this world. You just have to look hard to find the competitors."[3]

The most difficult, most risky new product category is leading-edge products. Developing leading-edge products is the dream of all SMMs and the "stuff" needed to make the cover of *Inc.* magazine. But these products require the greatest commitment of resources, and a lot of marketing experience, if they are to succeed.

The Saga of FLIR

The difficulty of developing leading-edge products is dramatically demonstrated in the development of the FLIR product described in Chapter 5. No matter how brilliant an idea or its technology is, a great deal of talent, money, and marketing savvy are needed to commercialize the product into something that customers can use.

In the case of the forward-looking infrared product that FLIR Systems marketed for use with helicopters, commercializing meant changing the existing ground-based energy product to an airborne, night-vision product for helicopter surveillance. This major new product development project included finding ways to get the new product certified by the FAA and then tested on a variety of helicopter applications involving extreme temperatures and vibration.

If at first you don't succeed ...   By 1980, Richard Sears, the founder of FLIR Systems, had managed to attract enough outside capital to develop the product for helicopters. After two years of working with the FAA, he finally received an experimental certificate that allowed him to test the new product for law enforcement, search-and-rescue, and military surveillance and reconnaissance applications.

As is true of most new high technology products, there were many unforeseen problems, and sales were not forthcoming. Sears was at a crossroads with the company and had to figure out a new approach to developing the product and markets.

After considerable soul searching, Sears decided his approach was wrong. He formed a new product team consisting of the sales manager, the heads of production and engineering, the chief financial officer (CFO), and himself. Reliance on customer and product information from the sales department wasn't working, because a good deal of information was verbal and the engineers were suffering from the usual "not-invented-here" syndrome. Sears told me, "The engineers' basic instincts were to inductively analyze problems, which often meant they would decide for the customer what was right based on the available data and their experience."[4]

Sears decided that if the product was to succeed, the team would have to get out to the customers in person. He made a rule that everyone on the team had to spend time with the customers, in their helicopters.

A customer-driven process.   Sears was determined that the customer was going to drive the product development process. He knew that his teammates would see customers' problems only by standing in their shoes. He designed a "customer contact sheet" that was used by everyone who met with a customer and that forced all team members to write down the data they collected in a uniform way. The idea was to identify customers' problems and needs well enough to convert them into sound product development.

The new approach worked well. The product development team quickly found out what it was going to take to make the new product work on a helicopter.

What the team found illustrates the large gap between brilliant engineering and workable products. For example:

- The products had been designed in a lighted lab. Nobody anticipated that the pilot would need the instrument's controls illuminated for night flying.
- Control knobs and switches were designed for use without gloves. These had to be changed because, the team was told, pilots needed to wear gloves during cold weather.
- The constant vibration of the helicopter caused many electrical problems, and many of the purchased connectors did not work.
- Nobody had given much thought to connecting the unit to the helicopter's electrical system. Electrical noise transients, which occurred commonly, knocked out the instrument, just as a power surge can knock out a personal computer.
- Finally, nobody had thought to add an instrument to show the pilot which way the FLIR was pointing relative to the helicopter. (In the lab, the workers manually aimed the device.)

The field collaboration with customers was a big success, and soon the team had gathered all the information they needed to redesign the product, making it reliable and practical. Competing with major aerospace competitors (Texas Instruments, Hughes Aircraft, and Honeywell), FLIR Systems won a large contract from the Coast Guard in 1983 and was on its way to success.

The secret of FLIR's success. According to Richard Sears, the secret of his team's success was shifting the product development focus from an internal, laboratory orientation to an external, customer orientation. He remarks:

> I had experienced, talented people, but it required developing skills in interviewing, listening, and observing to overcome the problems. Managing a team approach to developing new products is truly an adventure in social psychology, but it is the only way to maintain a balanced approach that focuses on the customer.

FLIR Systems grew from a small research company with $250,000 in sales in 1980 to a publicly held, midsize firm with revenues of $38 million in 1993. Today the company markets its products to customers all over the world.

THE 10-STEP PROCESS FOR ACHIEVING NEW PRODUCT SUCCESS

Are you willing to "bet the farm" on developing a high-risk, leading-edge product? Would your company be better off modifying an existing product? What about producing a replacement or substitute product? The 10-step process highlighted in Figure 6–4 and discussed below will help you make the right decision, one that will match your company's ambitions and capabilities. It will greatly improve your chances for success, by getting customers deeply involved in the process.

Step 1: Select a product development team. Earlier I discussed the problems that result when a solitary inventor creates a product without feedback from other people (including customers). One effective solution is to make sure that all new products are developed by a team rather than by a single person.

A team representing many different functions in the company will bring multiple viewpoints to the product development process right from the start. It will keep the project focused on customer needs and provide coordination with other company departments. This eliminates the problem of handing the new product to a department without prior knowledge and ensures connection to the outside world.

FIGURE 6–4
Customer-Driven Product Development

Step 1.   Select a product development team.

Step 2.   Develop new product ideas.

Step 3.   Screen the ideas.

Step 4.   Make a reality check: How much can you afford to gamble?

Step 5.   Define product attributes and customer benefits.

Step 6.   Identify target markets and customers.

Step 7.   Search for competitors.

Step 8.   Ask customers, prospects, and industry experts for their opinions.

Step 9.   Develop the product/service package.

Step 10. Build a prototype and get customer feedback.

In a very small company, the product development team might consist of a handful of people—the owner, an engineer, and someone in sales. In a larger company, you might choose a person from each department or each major function in the company to be on the team—an engineer or a designer, a sales or marketing person, a production or manufacturing person, someone from accounting or finance, and the project leader.

No matter how small or large the team, there must be a leader or product champion who has enough ambition and clout to keep the project moving. The team leader will have to be independent and have enough authority to hold the other team members' feet to the fire. This is critical, because by definition, each team member is going to bring a completely different viewpoint and set of skills into the process, and issues need to be resolved for progress. Team dynamics don't always work out, and sometimes a team member has to be removed. If the team leader does not have the authority to remove a member, he or she may have to depend on an outside board or even an investor to champion the cause.

The most important thing the team will do is to gather information about market and customer needs. Everyone should be involved in this phase of the process—sharing information, making customer calls, and hearing the same input on needs. This focus on customer needs should continue through the entire process.

Step 2: Develop new product ideas.   The first step the team will undertake is finding new product ideas. The best place to start is with customers. A survey similar to the examples described in Chapter 2 is an excellent way to find out about quality, service, and product deficiencies. If a customer takes the time to complain about anything related to the product or service, you are getting free product development information from the best expert in the marketplace.

Even lost order analysis discussed in Chapter 2 will provide good ideas for new products or product modifications. Product problems or deficiencies that result in lost orders represent possibilities for modified products, line extensions, and even brand-new products.

When enlisting customers in your new product development process, look for companies that are always trying to find ways to get more for their money or more performance from their products or processes. You need to search for customers who support innovation within their own companies, whether they are large or small. Customers often come up with their own new product ideas, or at least with innovations that you can use in the product development process.

If customers have a lot to gain from a product innovation, such as a higher-speed machine that puts out more products per hour and more shipments per year, they will make excellent collaborators because, by helping you, they will be helping themselves.

Fourteen sources of new product ideas.   Enlisting customers in your development process is one way to acquire new product ideas. Here are 14 other cost-effective methods for generating new product ideas:

1. *Technical publications.*   Read about new product releases in trade journals. These publications are an excellent place to begin the search for competitive products and may stimulate product ideas.

2. *Competitors.*   Develop a competitive matrix (described in Chapter 4) on your known competitors, and determine their product weaknesses.

3. *Suppliers.*   Spend some time with your suppliers' technical people talking about the materials and technology of the parts they are shipping you. Suppliers are always looking for new applications for their products, and will often come up with suggestions that lead to new products.

4. *Suggestion box.*   Implement a suggestion program for everyone in the company, and offer a prize or bonus to the employee who comes up with the best new product idea each month.

5. *Trade shows.* Make sure everyone in your company who attends trade shows is assigned a small project: to evaluate a competitor's products and report back to the company.

6. *Clipping service.* Pay a clipping service to send you specialized technical articles and new product ideas from specific trade journals.

7. *User panels.* Ask a group of key customers to visit your plant to discuss new product ideas.

8. *Customer survey.* Review the complaints and comments generated by customer surveys (described in Chapter 2).

9. *Service records.* Make sure that your service department documents all design problems and all customer complaints and suggestions.

10. *Patent files.* Research government patent files to find out what's on file for each competitor you find during the new product development phase. (This is simpler than you may think; see Chapter 4.)

11. *Hiring.* Hire industry experts or salespeople and engineers from competitor companies who are known to be innovative.

12. *Brainstorming sessions.* Bring together a group of employees, customers, suppliers, friends, relatives, and/or anyone else who has a creative mind to brainstorm new product ideas.

13. *Technical wizards.* Take outside engineers, scientists, inventors, or other technical wizards to lunch, and pick their brains for new product ideas.

14. *Competitors' products.* Buy competitors' products, and tear them down to find their weaknesses. Use the information you gain to design your own, better product.

Step 3: Screen the ideas. It's easy to get carried away with how wonderful your product idea is. Screening forces you to face the question, "What's in it for the customers?" This gets the customer into the game early on.

This step is crucial. Once projects get past the talking stage, they tend to generate their own momentum. After money has been spent and people take ownership of a product idea, changing the direction of the development process is difficult.

There are many ways to screen new product ideas, ranging from having the boss choosing his or her favorite idea to use of complex numerical rating scales.

Screening doesn't have to be complicated to be effective. All that's required is to get a group of knowledgeable people together to talk about potential product ideas from a variety of angles (marketing, engineering, manufacturing, finance, etc.)—and to do this before the ideas begin to cost a lot of money. A preliminary screening session will enable team members to prioritize the new product ideas and choose the ones that are worth more time and investigation.

Before the screening meeting begins, make preparations to facilitate the conversation and record the answers so they can be easily evaluated. You can use a notepad, a blackboard, a computer, or any other method you choose; the important thing is to organize the information into categories and ask penetrating screening questions.

The objective of the screening meeting is to find out why anyone would want to buy the product you propose. Begin with a description of the product idea, the customer need that exists, or the problem to be solved by the product. This will logically progress to a discussion of who might buy it.

Included in the discussion should be questions about customer benefits and why the product is unique. Figure 6–5 presents a screening matrix that includes some examples to ponder.

Step 4: Make a reality check—how much can you afford to gamble? Sensible gamblers know what game they want to play and how much they're willing to risk or lose. Before a new product idea takes on a life of its own, you need to determine whether it is compatible with your company's strengths and available resources. You must also decide how much the company wants to gamble on new product development.

The first thing to determine is whether your new product idea falls into the category of modified, substitute, or leading-edge product. Then ask some probing questions, such as the following:

1. Will the product be sold to existing customers, or will you have to find new customers and new markets? Especially if marketing is not your strong suit, please spend some time agonizing over this question.
2. Do you have a strong product champion who can lead a development team and push the product through the roller coaster of development problems?
3. How much money are you willing to spend on this project?

FIGURE 6-5
Screening Matrix

Describe the Idea	*What Is the Need or Problem?*	*Solutions Offered*	*Is the Idea Unique?*	*Who Will Buy the Product?*
A data-acquisition system that is small, battery-driven, and programmed in Basic.	Gather data at remote sites without power. Sites such as oil wells, weather stations, arctic plants, and ocean buoys, need to gather data that can be processed later by computer.	A microcontroller-type board with analog to digital board; the data unit with a battery could be enclosed in a watertight box. A modification of several existing products.	Don't know. There are hundreds of data-acquisition products available.	From previous quote activity, we think that there may be applications for the product in: • The military • Meteorological companies • The FAA • Oil companies These organizations will probably want custom versions. We don't know whether there are commercial possibilities for volume production.

4. Are enough resources (time, people, facilities, and money) available to develop this product all the way through to customer acceptance?

5. Is the technology required for developing the product within the understanding and skills of your people?

6. Can the product be developed within your existing manufacturing process, or will you have to invest money in tooling and new equipment?

7. Do you have any idea how much sales or profits the new product could generate in the first year?

8. Do the projected sales and profits justify the required expense and risk?

9. What are the minimum sales that the product will have to achieve in the first year in order to keep investors happy?

10. Can the product be sold through your existing sales force or channels of distribution?

11. Does the product fit or have synergy with the other product lines within the company?

12. Does the company have enough resources to continue the business even if the new product fails? (This is the most crucial question.)

If the answer to many of these questions is no, or if you find yourself thinking, "I don't know," stop and make a reality check of the situation. Find a quiet place where there won't be any phone interruptions and think seriously about the problematic questions for one hour.

Afterward, if your gut feeling is not good, either halt the product or spend some more time and money on market intelligence and customer interviews, until you are convinced the product has a good chance of succeeding.

Step 5: Define product attributes and customer benefits.   An acid test for determining whether a new product will meet customer needs during the screening process is to force the team to describe the product or service in terms of user benefits. Business customers are interested in products that provide solutions to their problems, and these solutions can often be measured in dollars. The question is, What unique attributes or benefits will your product offer a customer that will help the customer accomplish a task or solve a problem more cost-effectively than current products or methods?

As basic as this idea may sound, most small manufacturers describe their products in terms of product features and engineering specifications rather than solutions or end user benefits. The reason is that many sales-people have been trained to sell in either a sales-driven or a product-driven environment. They usually attempt to sell themselves, the features of the product, or the company.

In reality, business customers care little about product features, your company, or even the information you supply in your proposal, unless it relates to solving their problem or to the final outcome they have visualized in their minds.

Figure 6–6 presents a checklist that will help you and your sales force to redefine your products in terms of user benefits. As the checklist suggests, there are many ways to calculate payback, save time, or make an operation more efficient.

Choose one or two existing products, or a potential new product, and use the checklist to determine the end user benefits. Write a brief note next to each item that might apply.

If you are developing a new product and you find that you can't determine the user benefits, don't spend any more money until you can define them. Ask a few customers what they think the new product will do for them. Customers usually have some kind of payback formula to justify buying a product; with a little probing, you can find out what formula they use, and redefine your product to make it more salable.

Step 6: Identify target markets and customers.   Once you have defined user benefits, the next step is to make sure there is a group of customers (market niche) willing to buy the product. Choosing the right customers for the new product is one of the most important decisions you will make in the new product development process. This is a step that should be considered very carefully in terms of your resources and sales staff.

Many new products are based on great ideas but simply never find buyers. Having an idea of who the buyers will be before you spend a lot of money seems logical, but the reality is that a lot of small manufacturers don't believe in the target market idea. A more popular method is to invent a product and leave it up to the sales and advertising departments to find buyers, as I discussed earlier in this chapter. This approach can be extremely risky, depending on how much money the company has invested in the product and how much it knows about potential customers.

FIGURE 6–6
User Benefit Checklist

How will the new product save the customer money or reduce costs?

1. Reduced labor cost   _____
2. Reduced downtime   _____
3. Lower inventory costs   _____
4. Less storage expense   _____
5. Saving time in a service job   _____
6. Increased productivity   _____

Is the product higher in quality than existing products?

1. More reliable   _____
2. More dependable   _____
3. More durable (lasts longer)   _____
4. Improved product performance   _____

Does the new product offer more or better services?

1. Easier to maintain and service   _____
2. Improved production capacity   _____
3. Better technical support   _____

Following are three different customer/target market scenarios to consider. Each requires a different selling and marketing approach.

1. *Modified product sold to known customers.*   The sales strategy in this scenario is reasonably easy, because the customer knows the sales rep and the product. The sales rep can handle this situation with the usual engineering and service support services.

2. *Modified or substitute product sold to new customers.*   In this scenario the sales rep's job becomes more difficult. The new customers might be in the same industry or in another industry with different problems, needs, and applications. The new customers also might be large companies with totally different requirements and different decision-making units. (In Chapter 9, I'll discuss the unique problems involved in selling to large customers.)

   In this situation, the sales rep needs a lot of help in understanding the benefits of the product, and perhaps in making the initial sales calls. Qualified advertising inquiries to locate buyers and a good mailing list are also essential. Some effort is required to define and select target markets.

3. *Leading-edge products sold to new customers.* The sales rep in this scenario doesn't know the customers or markets, and the product is totally new. Extensive training, qualified inquiries, technical support, customer profiles, and target marketing are essential to successful selling in this situation.

Selecting a target group or groups of customers and defining their needs prior to the launch of the product really saves time and focuses the sales effort. As a minimum, select a target market niche, define the customers in the niche in terms of a four-digit SIC code, and then find out how many prospect companies are in the market area.

The bottom line is that you can dramatically increase your chances of finding enough buyers to justify the product costs if you spend enough time identifying customers and target markets.

Step 7: Search for competitors. As soon as the target markets are generally identified, assign a team member the task of looking for competitors. It is crucial to have someone on the team set aside time to look for competitors in order to avoid the me-too trap described earlier in this chapter. All team members should be convinced that as much time and enthusiasm must be devoted to this task as to designing the prototype, and that this task must be accomplished before very much money is spent on product development.

The objectives are to find all competitive products, to determine the number of competitors in the target market, and to discover the approximate prices of competitive products. I once asked a high technology client how many companies in the United States manufactured small industrial computers like his microcontrollers. He quickly answered that he had only one competitor in the United States.

A quick phone survey and literature search revealed 10 direct and more than 50 indirect or substitute competitors with several hundred different product models. My client had a hard time accepting that there were 10 direct competitors and an even harder time believing that the substitute products were competitors—even though his own customers were buying them. The lesson is that there are always more competitors and more substitute products than SMMs think.

The search for competitors can be done quickly and on a tight budget. It doesn't take a lot of time or money to find competitors, request their literature, and determine pricing, once the target markets have been determined (with the help of the competitive matrix discussed in Chapter 4).

Here's an example of a quick competitor search that I did for Gyro-corp, a small manufacturing client. The company had acquired a contract from the Army to build a special gyroscope with two degrees of freedom, which was to be used in an Army attack helicopter. After all the R&D money had been spent, the client wanted to know where else it might be able to sell the product, but the owner would allow me to spend only a few hours on a competitor search.

I searched directories and buyer's guides, including the *Thomas Register of Manufacturers* from the local library. I also did an on-line computer search, and I searched the US Department of Defense's microfiche records. I found 87 gyroscope manufacturers in the United States. Six were producing two-axis, directional gyroscopes with the ability to build a product exactly like my client's. The companies ranged in size from 55 to 5,000 employees.

Because the company had few resources and a slim marketing budget, Gyrocorp's owner wisely decided not to compete directly in the new gyroscope market, after I presented the results of my search. Instead, the company went after the repair and refurbishing market niche, which was not attractive to the big players in the game.

Devoting some time to uncovering competitors will provide your product designers with information and ideas for product advantages that the customers are not receiving from competitive products. The competitor search will not only prevent the failure of me-too products but will also help you to avoid the costs involved in having to modify your product before someone will buy it. It's a good example of spending pennies to save dollars.

Step 8: Ask customers, prospects and industry experts for their opinions. Obviously, the best way to find out what customers really want in a new product is to ask them. You can phone them, do a mail survey like the three customer surveys discussed in Chapter 2), or visit them in person. Telephone probes and personal visits are discussed below.

The telephone probe. Using the screening matrix shown in Figure 6–5, develop a few questions about why you think new prospects might buy the product. Then select 10 or 20 prospects and go over the questions with them. Make your questions open-ended and brief; all you want to do is gauge the prospects' reactions to your idea.

For instance, after explaining your idea for a new high-speed dipwhipper with PC controls and graphic displays, you might ask your customer or prospect the following questions:

1. What do you think of this idea?
2. Would it solve any problems you are having?
3. Is the product missing any important features or benefits?
4. What is the likelihood that you would buy a dipwhipper at a price of $10,000? At a different price?
5. What are your suggestions for modifying the product idea?

To get this program off the ground, commit to calling a different person in the industry every day. If you are not comfortable doing phone surveys, have a sales rep make the calls or hire an outsider to make them. Review all the information collected in the telephone surveys with the product development team, including criticism as well as positive comments.

Your telephone interviews will bring you new customer and market information everyday. The next step is to take your idea out to the market, and to allow customers and prospects to critique it, as Mentor Graphics did. If possible, take along a prototype, or at least some drawings or photos so that you can visually show the concept.

At this point, the inventor who gave birth to the idea or the technical people who are immersed in the technology will probably become sensitive, and dissension may haunt the team. However, it is absolutely vital to get valid customer information and opinions, particularly if they contradict the inventor's product vision.

Before I describe some techniques of visiting customers and prospects, let me digress briefly to discuss some of the personality problems that are present in all product development programs.

My friend Chuck Evans used to say that the business world is divided into three kinds of people: "People People, who like and seek feedback from others; Ideas People, who get a big bang out of new ideas; and Things People, who identify with and focus on things rather than people for their enjoyment and information resources."

I have spent most of my career working with and attempting to understand Things People, and I've concluded that they have some real disadvantages in developing new products, because of their built-in psychological biases. Here are some generalizations that apply to the Things People I have met:

They are usually introverts who are not comfortable with people and prefer to communicate with things (e.g., computers) or with other Things People. Their product ideas become deeply held beliefs that are quickly written in stone, and external feedback is looked on more as interference than as help. They often have a very hard time with customers (those people who can say whatever they want because they sign the checks), and they often confuse constructive criticism about a product or service with personal criticism.

The biggest shortcoming of Things People is that they often do not identify with or hear what customers say, which is a big problem in product development. This can lead to many problems that I group loosely under the title *mind reading*. Mind readers claim to know what customers need without having asked them.

For instance, an engineer who used to work for me always seemed to be able to make pronouncements about what customers would accept without talking to them. Whether it was a quotation, a change in production, a new product, or a service problem, this person always claimed to know in advance what the customers would accept. Of course, he was usually wrong.

I learned from this experience that some people simply don't relate to "people problems," particularly if they are allowed to operate exclusively in protected, noncustomer environments, such as engineering departments and R&D labs.

Mind reading seems to be a common trait of Things People. One of the best ways to deal with the problems caused by mind reading is to get the Things People out into the field and have them conduct personal interviews with customers. This allows them to see the customer's reality firsthand, instead of making up their own version of that reality.

Personal interviews.   As previously mentioned, it is essential that engineers, owners, and other important members of the team visit customers during the product development process. The people who visit your customers should have solid sales experience and should have developed good interviewing skills (see Chapter 3). If a team member doesn't have adequate interviewing skills, it's probably best to send along a person with good communication skills who can act as a "translator." At a minimum, the person who does the interviewing should have a thorough knowledge of the product idea and be able to discuss it in depth.

Personal interviews with end users are the single best way to test a product concept and to begin refining it. You might begin by developing a list of industry experts, such as trade magazine editors, association officials, and suppliers. Then you can set up a plan for interviewing these experts.

If there are industry people in your local area, commit to taking a different one out to lunch every week. This will make sure you and the team become attuned to customers and outside experts early on. Everyone has to take time to eat lunch or breakfast, so these calls shouldn't cut into your working hours.

When you talk to customers or industry insiders about your product ideas, ask them the same type of questions as those presented in "the Telephone Interview" in Chapter 3.

Step 9: Develop the product/service package.   The process of developing a successful new product should not be limited to the hardware aspect of the product. With some industrial products, the only way to achieve an advantage over competitors is to include additional services and benefits that appeal to the customer.

This step goes hand in hand with establishment of user benefits. Giving some thought to the service package while the new product is being developed will increase the chances of a successful new product launch. Sometimes a good service package can produce spectacular results even with a basic product.

A great example of a company that designed a unique product/service package is Safety-Kleen, a Wisconsin firm. This clever product was invented in a Wisconsin gravel pit, for the purpose of cleaning grimy truck wheel bearings in a sink with running solvent. It consists of a metal sink, a drum, and a submersible pump that draws solvent from the drum into the sink. The real competitive advantage of Safety-Kleen's product was that the users could exchange the dirty drums for clean ones; Safety-Kleen recycled the drums for the users.

Safety-Kleen was founded in 1968 and grew to $200 million in sales within 10 years, with a product that wasn't new or unique. What *was* unique was that Safety-Kleen found a way to clean the parts, take care of the solvent, and recycle the waste products at a very reasonable price. Others may have experimented with a similar idea, but no one had come up with a product/service package that was anything like Safety-Kleen's.

Adding the right services to the product is not as easy as it might appear. It requires an in-depth understanding of your customers' needs as well as your competition. Such an understanding may be acquired through a creative study of many combinations of services. Here is a list of some of the more popular services you may want to consider adding to your product:

1. *Design services.*   Plant layout drawings, presales service and advice, proposal drawings, vendor consultation programming help, and machine layouts or sketches are a few examples.

2. *Start-up services.*   These might include project coordination and management, installation, assembly, inspection, product testing, debugging, and start-up of equipment.

3. *Training and education.*   You might offer customer guidance and training on the application and adaptation of products, on-site demonstrations; user workshops, in-plant service training, safety advice, library services, and technical literature.

4. *Maintenance and repair services.*   Examples are cleaning, repairing, reconditioning, loaning equipment, maintenance services, troubleshooting services, and parts stocking.

5. *Emergency services.*   These might include toll-free 800 numbers for customer support, production downtime emergency services, overnight parts shipping, and a 24-hour hotline.

6. *Marketing services.*   You could offer joint or co-op advertising and promotions, sales engineering services, new product or applications development, joint market research, program updates, and sales aids.

7. *Financial services.*   Credit, leasing, renting, factoring, and discounting are examples of financial services that your customers may want.

8. *Miscellaneous services.*   Examples are trade-ins, dismantling, newsletters, application news, just-in-time delivery, consignment, and on-line information.

Step 10: Build a prototype and get customer feedback.
Companies spend a lot of time and money building prototypes without having their product ideas critiqued by outsiders. Then they move right into production. This means that the first serious reactions of the customer

occur at the point of sale. If the designers guessed wrong, the company is forced to modify the product.

Don't make the same mistake. Encourage a few of your MVCs to keep prototypes of your product in their plants for a few days, to play with them, and then to offer you their criticisms and suggestions for improvements. Choose MVCs who are "lead users"—who are usually the first to buy innovative new products. Their feedback can save you time, money, and headaches later on by preventing you from launching a product that's not yet ready for the market.

I used this technique with great success in one of my manufacturing jobs. Every time we designed a new production model of a palletizer machine, we offered to install the prototype on a consignment basis, with a 90-day free trial period. We agreed to provide all the service and engineering to make the machine run. We further agreed to make any necessary design or parts changes.

At the end of the trial period, customers could either pay for the machine or ask us to take it out of their plants, at our expense. This was a perfect way to get the customer's input in a real-life production situation. In *every case,* the customer kept the machine.

Involving the customer in the product at the prototype stage is challenging. Commitment and partnership are required to make it work. End users often don't know their needs until they are physically using the product, and their needs may continue to change right up to the end of the product development process. Constant communication and even negotiation are necessary so you can end up with a win-win situation and a successful product that can be sold to other companies.

I learned this during my first new product development project for a hydraulic crane manufacturer. I was a young product manager in charge of developing a line of hydraulic marine cranes that could be used on fishing vessels. After examining a lot of new product ideas and the many types of cranes and booms used on vessels, I decided to focus on a market niche in the tuna fishing fleet.

It was 1970, and the US tuna fleet was modernizing into a fleet of high-speed, efficient purse seiners that could travel anywhere in the world. Purse seiners use a net system that encircles a school of tuna. Once they catch up with a school of fish, they can be easily netted.

The problem was catching the school after it was sighted. The tuna fishermen had solved this problem by launching speedboats that could overtake schools of fish and head them off. Some of the more aggressive captains wanted to experiment with hydraulic cranes that could quickly launch and retrieve the speed boats, and I spent a lot of time in San Diego, California, listening to their needs and suggesting ideas for a new marine crane design.

We finally got a chance to build three prototypes for installation on a brand new 225-foot vessel. After trial runs in San Diego, the vessel left to fish off Mexico and would eventually travel through the Panama Canal to fish off the coast of western Africa.

I was concerned about the prototypes because we didn't know what structural problems might arise in rolling seas. Halfway through the cruise off Mexico, I received an urgent call from the ship captain, who told me that a cylinder rod on the main boom of the prototype had bent during a storm. He wanted to know what I was going to do about it.

I hopped on a plane with our service engineer and we flew overnight to Panama City to meet the vessel as it went through the canal. The captain set up a tarp over the crane so that we wouldn't burn our fair skins under the equatorial sun, and we completely disassembled and rebuilt the damaged crane in one day.

The two days we spent on the ship gave us time to commiserate with the captain and his maintenance crew about design weaknesses and suggestions for design changes that they would want on future marine cranes. On the basis of their experience, they suggested a completely different design for the boom swing mechanism, as well as stronger cylinder rods and hydraulic changes. We took a cylinder rod home, and metallurgical analysis showed that the crew members were right. We made the change to a high-alloy stainless steel.

Collaboration with the customer as a design partner, combined with a program of continuous design refinements, resulted in well-tested prototypes and the successful adoption of our cranes by other fishing companies in the fleet.

*   *   *   *   *

Most of the reasons for new product failures have to do with not paying attention to customers, markets, and competitors. This chapter has suggested some practical ways to avoid these mistakes by getting customers into the new product game, evaluating competitors early in the process, and finding out what the market wants. Once the new product is ready to be introduced to the market, the SMM must decide on the best method of distributing it. Chapter 7 will review a variety of distribution channel alternatives.

KEY POINT

The best consultant, adviser, designer, and market expert for new product development is the customer. If you approach your customers early in your product development process and keep them involved throughout the process, you will significantly increase your chances of success.

SUGGESTED ACTION

Photocopy "the New Product Game" (Figure 6–3), and pass it around the company. Ask employees to circle the problems they feel are negatively affecting your product development process. Develop a plan for acting on their suggestions.

NOTES

1. Robert G Cooper, "Why New Industrial Products Fail," *Industrial Marketing Management,* April 1975, pp. 315–26.
2. Interview with Kathy Wakefield, May 1993.
3. Interview with Ralph Shaw, April 1993.
4. Interviews with Richard Sears, January to July 1993.

Chapter Seven

Selecting the Most Effective Distribution Channels

Once a product has been developed, the SMM faces the task of finding the most efficient and the most effective way of distributing it. The choice of distribution channels varies according to the product being sold. The type of channel that sells a standardized product or subcomponent (on the lefthand side of the product range; see Figure 6–1) is very different from the channel that sells engineered systems requiring capital funding (on the righthand side of the range.) The selling approach, technical knowledge, services, and tasks required are very different.

For example, some manufacturers of products on the righthand side of the product range use highly trained technical specialists with engineering degrees, while manufacturers of products on the lefthand side may use distributors with minimal education and training. Most of the examples in this chapter focus on companies that sell technical and engineered products.

TRADITIONAL CHANNELS OF DISTRIBUTION

The traditional channel choices for SMMs are manufacturers' reps, distributors (dealers), and direct salespeople. These choices are discussed below.

Manufacturers' Reps

Manufacturers' reps are also known as **agents, brokers,** or **commissioned merchants,** or simply as **reps** (a generic term for any commissioned sales intermediary). They are found in almost every industry, and they often substitute for direct salespeople. Reps generally sell a narrow line of noncompeting products, do not take title to the goods, get paid on commission, and seldom stock inventory.

The major advantage of using reps is that the costs involved are variable rather than a fixed, since reps are not paid unless and until they sell something. They are also self-motivated, because they are independent businesspeople. Furthermore, turnover is lower with reps than with direct salespeople. They are usually the best channel choice to cover widely scattered accounts and are the easiest of all channels to set up.

The main disadvantage of using reps is the company's inability to control their time and sales coverage, because they are independent. A common criticism of reps is that they "sell what is selling."

Distributors

Distributor is a generic term for a variety of intermediaries who resell products. Distributors are also known as **wholesalers, dealers, importers, brokers, franchises,** or **merchants.** Depending on the products they resell, distributors can range from **supply houses** which carry inventory for local customers, to **specialized distributors,** who provide engineering, installation, and other technical services for a limited number of products. **Value-added distributors** are specialized, limited-line distributors who assemble or engineer different products into systems for the end user.

Distributors sell a wide range of products, carry inventories, and take title to the goods. They get paid on a discount (i.e., they buy goods at a discounted price). They often provide service and installation, and they can set their own prices and terms.

One major advantage of distributors is that they are a ready-made sales force. They provide manufacturers with quick market entry, and they have experience with local market conditions and customers. In addition, they can provide local inventory, sales, and service. Using distributors is a fast and cost-effective way to reach a large number of end users.

The main disadvantage of using distributors is that it's difficult for the manufacturer to control their time and sales coverage, because they serve many masters. Another disadvantage is that they usually require considerable factory promotion and support before they will spend much time on your product. Furthermore, full-line distributors don't do well with products that require technical selling; they simply don't have the time to become experts on a wide variety of products.

Factory Salespeople

Factory salespeople, as the name implies, are full-time employees of the manufacturer. They are also known as **direct salespeople.**

Factory salespeople sell their company's products (and only these products) directly to end users and sometimes to dealers. They usually get paid a salary and commissions.

Since factory salespeople are full-time employees of the manufacturer, they can devote all their time to selling specific products and accounts, and they can develop in-depth technical knowledge of their products.

Factory salespeople are most often used by larger companies that can afford the cost. In addition, they are used when the end user demands specialized (nonsales) services that independent reps can't afford to handle. They are also commonly used to sell technical products that require extensive training, knowledge, and education.

The major advantage of factory salespeople is that the manufacturer has 100 percent control of their time and sales coverage. Theoretically, factory salespeople have closer contact with customers and more expertise in products and applications, simply because they can devote all their time to one product line.

The main disadvantage of using factory salespeople is the high fixed costs involved, since factory salespeople are not paid strictly on commission. It also takes a long time and considerable investment to build, train, and manage a factory sales force.

ALTERNATIVE DISTRIBUTION CHANNELS

Business marketers in the 1990s are beginning to accept the fact that traditional markets have been subdivided into many niches composed of distinct groups of customers who want different products, prices, and services. Selling costs are rising too fast to justify serving these fragmented markets via traditional distribution channels. As a result, SMMs are being forced to change channels.

Several other trends are challenging the conventional thinking of SMMs and forcing them to develop creative approaches to selling and distribution:

- *Time constraints.* With the downsizing of large corporations, there are fewer people doing more work. This makes it more difficult for the SMM to spend time with buyers in face-to-face sales calls.

- *Voice mail.* For all the advantages of voice message systems, there is also a downside to them. Some customers use them strictly as a screening device and have no intention of returning calls. In many instances, these systems make getting an appointment or networking into a large company harder rather than easier.
- *JIT inventory.* Customers who use JIT systems are forcing dealers and distributors to carry more inventory, thus boosting their costs of doing business.
- *Total quality management (TQM).* Companies that adopt TQM programs are requiring vendors to undergo quality certification. If you wish to do business with these companies, it doesn't matter what channel or sales strategy you use if your company is not certified.
- *Postsale support.* Customers are demanding more choices, and manufacturers are modifying their product or service packages in order to gain competitive advantage. As a result, resellers are having to respond to more and more requests for after-sale support services, particularly for high-technology and engineered products.
- *Market direction.* In a fast-changing marketplace, independent salespeople need more direction and more support from their principals regarding target customers, priority market niches, and their role in product and market development.

In light of these trends, it's clear that the successful distribution strategies of the past may not work in the future. Many SMMs are already experimenting with a variety of new strategies in order to keep costs down while retaining the flexibility and depth they need to stay competitive (see Figure 7–1).

Some manufacturers have experimented with nontraditional channels such as catalogs, mail order, and telemarketing. Some companies are using a combination of channels. For example, many firms that have traditionally used factory salespeople are now experimenting with rep and distributor combinations to reach niches at a lower cost of sale. These new combinations are called *hybrid systems.*

Hybrid distribution systems are creative attempts to find a more efficient combination of methods to achieve the best sales coverage at the lowest cost, and to cover more market niches with a variety of channels. They are the wave of the future, according to *Harvard Business Review,* which predicts that hybrid systems will be "the dominant design of marketing systems in the 1990s."[1]

FIGURE 7–1
Old and New Channel Solutions

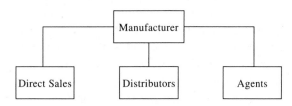

Traditional Channels of Distribution

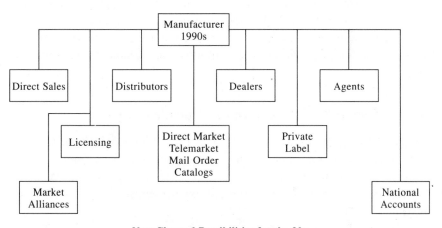

New Channel Possibilities for the 90s

Hybrid combinations of factory salespeople, reps, and distributors are already being used by large manufacturers, but SMMs are also beginning to experiment with new possibilities. Some examples are described below.

Converting Factory Salespeople to Independent Reps

In an effort to cut costs and improve coverage, some manufacturers have taken a "have your cake and eat it too" approach by converting factory salespeople to rep firms. This approach gives the SMM the benefit of sales representation by factory-trained people, at a variable cost.

A good example of this arrangement is provided by a manufacturer of architectural and building materials products. The factory sales staff in the regional office had to cover widely dispersed end users of specialized building products. This required driving long distances to call on customers, which resulted in high selling costs.

During the recession of the early 1990s, the company decided that the volume in one of its territories was too small to justify an in-house sales force. It offered the manager of the sales office an exclusive contract to represent the company's product line if he would set up an independent rep company. The manager agreed.

The new company was able to pick up complementary product lines from other manufacturers, which helped it to generate more sales from fewer customers. It was a win-win situation because the manufacturer continued to receive orders from the territory, but at a lower selling cost, while each salesperson in the newly independent firm increased his or her income substantially through the addition of complementary product lines.

Factory Salespeople and Independent Reps

Many SMMs that traditionally used factory salespeople have watched their markets decline and divide into smaller market segments. Often these market segments aren't large enough to justify the high cost of a factory sales force, and companies are experimenting with new sales approaches.

For example, Buffalo Tank, a steel fabricating division of Bethlehem Steel, experienced declines in its markets in the mid-1980s. It was obvious that selling costs did not justify expanding the company's sales force to cover many small market niches. Bob Davidson, the division manager, recognized the advantages of channel segmentation, after he attended a seminar. He began selective recruitment of specialized manufacturing reps to complement or replace factory sales engineers.

The company decided to select specialized reps for specific market targets in given trading areas, and to retain a factory sales force for other areas. For the New England area, the company recruited three different manufacturing reps, whose specialties were the process industries; the power industry; and heating, ventilating, and air conditioning. Each rep was given an exclusive contract to handle specific products for the designated market only, and the same sales approach was used in other territories.

Soon afterward, Buffalo Tank was sold. The new general manager, Keith Osborne, continued the distribution strategy implemented by the previous management. The strategy was successful: by mid-1987, the company had increased sales sharply in selected niches, and profitability was restored.[2]

Factory Salespeople and Distributors

Columbia Steel Casting Company in Portland, Oregon, manufactures wear parts for crushers and other heavy equipment. The company grew rapidly by using factory salespeople selling to end users. As the company developed more product lines, reaching all end users with only the in-house sales force became increasingly difficult. The company decided to use independent dealers to work with the factory salespeople, who served as district managers.

Adding independent dealers to a factory sales force that formerly did most of the selling inevitably created tensions. According to Jack Mc-Nally, dealer sales manager for Columbia Steel Casting:

> We decided to use independent dealers to sell our line of crusher wear parts and make our factory salesmen district managers because we could reach more end users faster. There are always going to be problems in using independent dealers or reps, because they are independent businesses with many companies to satisfy, and they have to do what they need to do to stay in business. But dealers can stock inventory and provide local services to end users for us. This saves us a lot of money and gets us to more people. All in all, it was a good decision. Despite the control and territory issues, we couldn't have grown to where we are today without adding our dealer organization.[3]

Direct Marketing

One of the biggest factors driving the move to new distribution channels is the need to contain costs. Selling costs often represent 10 percent of sales revenues. Customers who are low-volume or geographically distant are becoming too expensive to reach through any of the rep, distributor, or direct sales force combinations outlined above. Many business marketers are using direct marketing channels to reach these marginal accounts.

The Direct Marketing Association defines *direct marketing* as "an interactive system of marketing which uses one or more advertising media to effect a measurable response and/or transaction at any location."[4]

Although direct marketing has long been the domain of consumer marketers, business marketers are also employing direct marketing as both a marketing technique and sometimes as a separate sales channel. Direct marketing techniques work for SMMs, distributors, and rep firms because in most cases they dramatically reduce selling costs. Several national surveys show cost reductions in the neighborhood of 5 percent to 25 percent, but results depend on the type of product and the type of channel.

Following are examples of how business marketers are employing direct marketing strategies, ranging from simple mail order and catalogs to more sophisticated direct mail and telemarketing follow-up systems.

Catalogs.   With the cost of face-to-face sales calls ranging from $75 to $500 and still rising, business-to-business catalogs (which cost roughly $1 to $5 each) are being used more and more to close business-to-business sales. By using knowledgeable inside salespeople and providing good technical and engineering support, it is possible to handle both presales information and order-closing activity through these catalogs.

Business catalogs come in a variety of forms, including brochures, three-ring binders, bound books, and even videotapes.

A major advantage of business catalogs is that they provide the printed specifications and pricing information which buyers need to initiate the purchase process. Also, when there are multiple buyers or specifiers in the loop, the initial contact may need catalogs to show to superiors and other decision makers or to accompany a request for funds.

Catalogs are used to respond to advertising inquiries, for distribution at trade shows, as mailers to reps and distributors, and as collateral information to pass out to sales prospects. Innovative manufacturers have designed catalogs that are integral parts of a telemarketing system. Others are using catalogs as a separate mail order channel to replace other uneconomical channels and to reduce selling costs. Distributors are also beginning to publish their own catalogs as a supplementary channel of distribution.

Catalog systems are now regularly used to sell computer hardware and software products, material handling equipment, safety products, aftermarket parts, office equipment, and many other types of business products. The key to successful use of catalogs seems to be standard products that can be inventoried and easily shipped. Successful catalog marketing also requires up-to-date, well-maintained mailing lists and the establishment of toll-free phone numbers to make it easy for customers to order.

Telemarketing. Another direct marketing technique closely allied to use of catalogs and direct mail is **telemarketing,** which is also called **inside phone sales, business development,** and **telesales.** Systematic use of the telephone for selling has come into its own as a business-to-business sales technique.

Even manufacturers of technical products and capital equipment have begun to use a direct marketing approach that includes telemarketing, direct mail, and catalogs to handle accounts that cannot be cost-effectively managed by field salespeople.

Hampton Power Products: A telemarketing success story. Chuck Martin is president of Hampton Power Products, Inc., a distributor of power transmission equipment. In 1987, Martin was using three field salespeople to cover a four-state area, but he didn't believe that a field sales force was the most cost-effective way to handle all the accounts in his territory. When he took a close look at the field sales effort, he found three problems:

1. Field salespeople were responsible for prospecting and calling on some 350 accounts, making it physically impossible to work with all of them.[5]
2. "Insides sales was viewed as a cost of doing business."[6] Inside sales handled support and service tasks, but was not responsible for contributing to sales and profits.
3. Field salespeople were paid 20 percent of the gross profit of each sale. With selling costs averaging $120 per call, the salespeople could not afford to call on low-volume accounts.

Martin spent a lot of time researching the literature on telemarketing, and documenting what other companies had tried. Among other things, he discovered that many telemarketing efforts were not successful, for the following reasons:

- Telemarketers handled sales, service, parts, engineering, proposal, and other support tasks and did not have time to focus on selling or specific tasks.
- Telemarketers had inadequate internal support, information, and materials to do the job.

- Compensation was low and provided little incentive.
- There was no well-thought-out plan of action or division of responsibilities.
- Outside salespeople perceived the telemarketing program as a threat and worked to scuttle it.
- Management lacked commitment to the program and did not have the patience to work out the bugs.
- Telemarketers were not trained to sell the features and benefits of the company or product.
- Telemarketers were not trained to handle customer objections and complaints, nor were they able to explain policies.

Once he understood these problems, Martin developed a business plan for creating a completely self-sustaining telemarketing department that would handle small accounts, prospect for new accounts, and qualify prospects and leads so that the field salespeople could concentrate their time on larger accounts. The resulting telemarketing system at Hampton Power Products involves more than inside salespeople with telephones. It is a sophisticated computer system that includes a database and special telemarketing software (Figure 7–2).

As Figure 7–2 shows, the telemarketing system consists of a centralized database on which a variety of customer, product, and other information is maintained. The figure shows how tasks are distributed between inbound and outbound telemarketing. All telemarketers have easy access to any information in the database, which they can call up while they are talking on the phone to customers and prospects.

The system software enables the telemarketers to automatically send appropriate information to customers and prospects, with the push of a few buttons. The system also makes it easy for them to compile forecasts, sales data, and other management reports.

The telemarketers handle low-volume accounts by themselves, and work with the field sales force to manage certain other accounts. They are paid a salary plus commissions, which vary depending on the type of account and whether or not they share responsibility for the account with a field salesperson. All accounts that are developed by the telemarketing department into larger-volume accounts are turned back over to the field sales force.

Initially the members of the field sales force were suspicious of the new telemarketing department. But it didn't take long for them to figure

FIGURE 7–2
Telemarketing System—Hampton Power Products Inc.

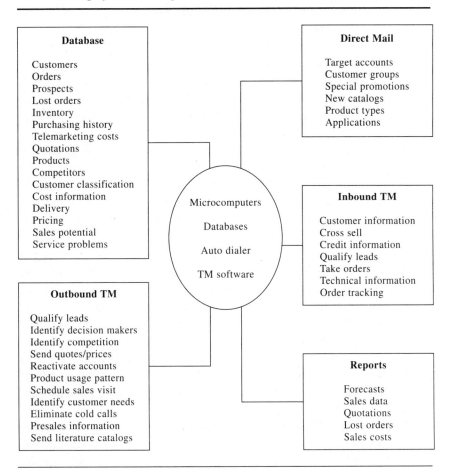

out that the system was honest and well-thought-out, and to recognize that being supported by the telemarketing department helped them in many ways.

The telemarketing department worked better than anyone would have predicted. The department paid for itself within the first six months of operation, and by 1992 it was responsible for 13 percent of the total company sales. The department had found and developed 46 new accounts by then, or about one-third of all new business developed by the company. At $6 per telemarketing call versus $120 for a field sales call, the company has realized tremendous savings while maintaining a high level of responsiveness to customers.

Climax Portable Machine Tool Company.   There are many examples of SMMs that have reduced selling costs and supported a field sales organization with telemarketing, as Hampton Power Products has done. Some companies have developed direct marketing systems so powerful that they are capable of handling the entire sales effort.

Climax Portable Machine Tool Company, based in Newberg, Oregon, is a small manufacturer of portable machine tools, ranging from a $1,700 clamp-on milling machine that cuts new keyways to a $150,000 machine with computer numerical controls (CNCs). The products are offered to a variety of geographically scattered customers, from paper mills to power plants.

During the 1970s, Climax used a field sales organization consisting of independent reps and multiline supply house distributors. Neither reps nor distributors worked well as a channel of distribution because the Climax products were a minor product line competing with many other lines. Selling costs were too high, and the company was not doing a good job of penetrating its target markets.

In 1979, Climax developed an inquiry follow-up system written in BASIC language that made use of a database and ran on a minicomputer. The system was simply designed to process inquiries into a database, and all follow-up work was handled on paper.

The program worked, and the company began using telemarketing as part of its sales efforts. Within a couple of years the original software had been perfected into a direct marketing system so efficient and effective that it replaced all the company's US reps and distributors.

In 1984, Climax converted to a new system, using software with programmed fields that prompted the operator through the sales steps. This new system offered the first automatic follow-up system.

In 1988, a telemarketing inquiry system (TIS) was installed. Its software had pull-down windows that helped telemarketers to move through the sales steps efficiently. In 1990 the system was converted to a local area network (LAN) system that replaced the terminals with individual PCs.

The current telemarketing system is designed around a seven-step selling process, which qualifies each lead or new prospect in terms of level of interest and potential for future projects. The process begins when the sales engineer loads all required information about the prospect into the database; a catalog and a personal letter are then automatically mailed. The software system prompts the salesperson through each of the seven selling steps, and he or she types in the answers. The sales session ends with the prospect being classified into one of 10 status categories for future telemarketing action, such as "A new inquiry that has not been contacted by phone" (status 1) and "Owners of Climax tools with potential for more purchases" (status 7).

Climax supports the telemarketing effort by generating 10,000 to 12,000 leads per year through aggressive trade journal and direct response card advertising. Catalogs are sent to all respondents along with any other information that it takes to close the sale, including engineering drawings, videos of working tools, application information and specifications, prices, and formal quotations. The telemarketing system even works for RFQs on capital projects that require months or even years to get funding approvals. A service and engineering department supports the sales effort with field installation, operation, and repair services.

Gordon Martin, marketing communications manager, says that the telemarketing system has significantly reduced selling costs and improved sales. The company occasionally meets customers at trade shows and still does some on-site demonstrations, but Martin says that, except for overseas distributors, almost all sales are consummated by phone. The "problem" of not meeting the customer face-to-face does not seem to be a problem; repeat business is common, and the company has established good relationships with more than 4,000 customers. Climax now sells 25 different products to a wide range of US companies and also direct-markets to Canada and Mexico.

CHOOSING THE APPROPRIATE CHANNELS

It takes some experimenting for an SMM to determine which of the channel alternatives described above will be the most efficient and cost-effective in its own situation. The possibilities of reducing selling costs and improving sales and customer satisfaction are great, but (there is always a "but") adding or changing channels will present a whole new set of control problems, and it is important to consider the issues involved. Before adding or changing channels, the SMM should answer the following four questions:

1. What can we afford?
2. What marketing direction do we want to take?
3. What level of sales coverage do we expect?
4. Should we use independent reps or factory salespeople and distributors?

These questions—and ways to find the answers to them—are discussed below.

What Can We Afford?

All discussions about selecting the correct channels should begin with a determination of what the company can afford. Discussions about the advantages of factory salespeople versus independent channels are academic if the cost of an in-house sales force can't be justified.

Cost of sale.   There are several ways to calculate the costs of various distribution channels. The cost-of-sale method is widely used. This method doesn't take into consideration product complexity or the quantity sold, but it is a useful tool in generally aligning the appropriate channel by price.

Many companies use 10 percent of the selling price as a general allowance to support each sale. According to a study by McGraw-Hill, selling and marketing costs (including marketing communication, direct selling, and marketing support costs) average 8.9 percent across a wide variety of industries. Some industries, such as electronics and computers, have considerably higher sales or marketing costs, but 10 percent seems to be a good rule-of-thumb estimate.[7]

Suppose a factory salesperson sold a $3,000 product. At a 10 percent cost of sale, this would allow approximately $300 to cover salary, commissions, benefits, and travel expenses—if the product could be sold in a single visit. If it took six sales calls to sell the $3,000 product, then only $50 ($300÷6) would be available per call—clearly not enough money to cover the selling expenses of a direct salesperson. In this case, a less costly distribution channel would be needed.

If the product were a $200,000 production machine, a 10 percent cost of sale would be $20,000. This would probably support a direct salesperson flying around the country and making many sales calls.

The breakeven point.   Another way to gauge the cost of a distribution channel is by determining the amount of sales required to break even. At a 10 percent cost of sale, if a direct salesperson covering a large sales territory cost the company $100,000 a year, the rep would have to produce $1 million in sales for the company to break even.

This would require a product with a high selling price or large volumes. Paying an independent rep a commission is much more practical if the revenues won't support the selling costs, or if there is no hard evidence that the territory can consistently produce at least $1 million in sales.

Sell price.   In their book, *Business Plans that Win $,* Stanley Rich and David Gumpert suggest that channels can be categorized by selling prices.[8] Figure 7–3 suggests some product-channel possibilities. For instance, a product with a price of $300 may require a distributor or direct mail technique because of the high cost of sale relative to the low cost of the product. At the other extreme, a $200,000 system can justify many face-to-face sales calls to a remote plant, and executive-level selling.

Although the sell price and channel suggestions highlighted in Figure 7–3 are simple rules of thumb, they do point out some of the problems of SMMs that sell a wide variety of products with a variety of selling prices. Figure 7–4 presents an example of a hydraulics distributor that uses direct

FIGURE 7–3
The Sell Price Rule

Typical Sell Price	Typical Channel
Less than $1,000	Mass distribution
$1,000–$10,000	Independent reps (agents)
$10,000–$100,000	Factory sales force
$100,000 plus	Executive sales

FIGURE 7–4
Cost-of-Sale Estimate

Description	Sell Price	Possible Channel
Seal kit	$ 10	Distributor
Software	200	Catalog
Portable tools	500	Telemarketing
Custom tanks	5,000	Reps (agents)
Crusher castings	25,000	Direct sales
Packaging system	200,000	Executive or direct sales

salespeople to sell a product line ranging from $10 hydraulic seal kits to $15,000 pumping systems. The pump system price will support many sales calls, but the seal kit doesn't justify even a single personal visit.

Here the possibility of a variety of channels exists. For instance, the seal kit could be sold in quantity by a distributor because of its low selling price and sales expense allowance. The low-price and small-volume orders could be handled by an inside telemarketing salesperson.

What Marketing Direction Do We Want to Take?

For the independent sales channel to have a reasonable chance of succeeding in a changing marketplace, the factory has to do a good job of providing information and leads from selected market niches. This information helps the independent sales organization to set sales priorities, to find new customers through qualified leads, and to focus its selling time.

On the other hand, if the small manufacturer's primary marketing strategy is shotgunning and there is little or no focus on market niches or target accounts, the independent channel is automatically in trouble. In this situation, the marketing responsibilities are implicitly transferred to the channel, which is supposed to find ways of getting orders without market direction, and, most of the time, without market support. It's virtually impossible for the sales channel, however good, to succeed in this environment.

What Type and Level of Sales Coverage Do We Expect?

What do you expect the sales channel to do in order to cover a given territory? Sales coverage, or the lack of it, is the reason for termination of many independent sales agreements, so you must lay out your expectations in advance.

When a SMM's attitude is "Any sale is a good sale" (the attitude that prevails in classic shotgunning), there are no rules for sales coverage. The result is often a stormy marriage, in which both parties constantly haggle over priority accounts, product and market development calls, cherry picking of the easiest sales, and commitment of time to the products.

Sales coverage for the SMM with a marketing plan and specific target markets is a very different game. A progressive manufacturer is going to want new markets explored, target accounts covered, new products promoted, and considerable time spent on market feedback and competitor information—the same things they would expect from a direct salesperson.

I suggest that sales coverage should also include the following factors: leads generated by the factory and followed up by the rep, telemarketing calls, quotations, orders, target account coverage, market and product development calls, sales reports, periodic quotation reviews, and, of course, the sales forecast.

Should We Use Independent Reps or Factory Salespeople and Distributors?

Manufacturers' relationships with independent reps cannot be the same as their relationships with factory salespeople. Independent sales organizations are just that—independent. They have their own business goals and requirements. There are built-in differences that can lead to tensions and even an adversarial relationship unless the independent channel is treated as a business partner.

The Pareto Principle (the 80/20 Rule) applies to relationships between manufacturers and independent sales channels. Probably 20 percent of these relationships are excellent, but the other 80 percent range from mediocre relationships in which both parties seem to just go through the motions, to stormy marriages that lead to divorces. A relationship is usually only as good as the weaknesses of both parties and their ability to communicate.

The following parody is based on real-life experiences, and is meant to illustrate the typical weaknesses and tensions of relationships between manufacturers and independents.

Burt Broadhead versus Rich Raven. Burt Broadhead, the president of Dynamic Fillers, is a second generation owner of a family-owned machinery manufacturing company. Burt grew up in the business, working in the machine shop during the summers while attending engineering school. Like his father the machinist, Burt is a technical guy who is most comfortable with tangible things that can be milled or drilled. Burt is not comfortable with intangible concepts such as marketing or planning. He views sales reps as necessary evils and suspects that many would sell their mothers into slavery for an order. Burt considers himself a People Person, but the independent agents he uses drive him crazy.

Dynamic Fillers has had good years and bad years, but profitability always seems to be elusive. Because of cash flow problems, Burt is always pushing for more sales, and he doesn't understand why the reps don't spend more time on his product. Burt is always developing new products for the reps to peddle, and he spends a fortune exhibiting his equipment at the industry's big trade show in Chicago. He doesn't really believe that advertising leads turn into sales, and he feels that marketing is what he is paying the reps to do.

Burt drives a big Cadillac, drinks and eats too much, and is on the fast track to an obligatory midlife crisis. At the most recent sales meeting, he had one too many martinis and was overheard to say:

> The only way reps can be successful is to get into their cars and spend a lot more time face to face with their customers. Most of our reps spend all their time on the phone, simply cherry picking their territories to get the most sales for the least effort. I can't wait until Dynamic is big enough to afford our own direct salespeople.

Rich Raven is a rep for Dynamic Fillers and nine other related machinery companies. Rich is the second-generation president of Raven Packaging, a family-owned manufacturers' rep firm. He earned a business degree at State University to please his parents. (He really wanted to be a professional musician.)

Rich is disorganized and really doesn't understand what it takes to satisfy the principals. He regularly puts in 60-hour weeks and often gets up at 3:00 AM to be able to make an appointment in a distant city by 8:00 AM.

Rich, like many seasoned manufacturers' reps, has developed a healthy sense of paranoia about principals. He is fond of retelling a story about how one principal has fired Raven Packaging four times within 10 years. Rich is a driven person who is used to living on the edge, constantly fearful that politics will change and Raven Packaging will fall out of favor with a principal. During his perpetual struggle to hang onto or replace product lines, he has heard most of the criticisms of rep firms, such as:

- Reps spend time on everybody's product but mine.
- Reps are only interested in quick dollars and easy orders.
- Reps always go for the easy sale and won't do any prospecting or market development.
- Reps are not loyal to our company or our products. They sell what's easiest to sell.

Rich admitted:

Some of these criticisms are based on truth. We are part-time salespeople working for a number of taskmasters. Since no one else is going to pay the mortgage, we have to focus on getting orders, not developing markets.

Rich confessed that his worst fear is that his company will invest a lot of time and money in learning the products and developing the accounts of a manufacturing firm, and then one day lose all its investment because the factory decides to sell direct or terminate the agreement. He said:

Every time we seem to build up the sales of a territory to the point where we are really enjoying some repeat business, the factory appoints a factory salesperson or declares a house account and we start all over.

"This happens often," Rich added, "and causes reps to become very negative about representation. For every generalization they have about reps, we have one about principals." For example, Rich noted:

- Principals seldom provide enough good leads to help us focus our face-to-face selling time.
- Many principals don't have a marketing program; they expect us to develop one for them.
- The principal's sales managers change faster than the weather. Just about the time we've established a working relationship, they appoint a new guy and we start over.

- The principal isn't loyal to us and will forever play the game of hiring and firing firms to get sales coverage. They want us to invest time in becoming product experts, but they won't give us any long-term guarantees or contracts.
- They want us to do missionary calls on new products and new markets without compensation, but they criticize us when orders fall off because we're spending time in this area.

The Rich Raven and Burt Broadhead stories are not unusual. The criticisms they raise show that it takes a real commitment and understanding on both sides to make the marriage work.

In my experience, very few SMMs achieve the kind of sales and market success they want and need with independent sales channels. The reasons are false expectations, poor communication, and the fact that no one really examines what it will take to do the job.

How to Make the Marriage Work

Even though there are some disadvantages involved, using independent channels may become even more popular in the 1990s as sales costs continue to rise. If the reality is that an SMM cannot afford direct sales people or that certain market niches don't justify them, independent channels can be a viable alternative, when they are properly managed and supported.

Avoid false expectations.   To avoid false expectations and begin a relationship positively, it is necessary to define the markets carefully and break the selling job down to the tasks required. The factory and the independent sales channel need to take the time to evaluate each other's performance annually, to make sure that the required tasks are being performed on both sides and the partnership is working. In fact, I suggest that the evaluation and the defined tasks become part of the contract.

Reps should have a formal, objective, and perhaps even confidential way of evaluating the factory's efforts every year. Normally, independent sales organizations are so afraid of losing the line that they tend not to make waves, even when they are not being supported. The factory also allows the marriage to go on well beyond the time that the first problems show up, and neither side tends to resolve or communicate about basic issues until the marriage is on the rocks.

FIGURE 7–5
Distributor Performance Scale

Rate a distributor that currently represents your company on a scale of 1 (awful) to 10 (superb)

1. Focus on the right market niches	1 2 3 4 5 6 7 8 9 10
2. Complementary product lines	1 2 3 4 5 6 7 8 9 10
3. Understanding of how the market buys	1 2 3 4 5 6 7 8 9 10
4. Responsiveness to leads and quotations	1 2 3 4 5 6 7 8 9 10
5. Ability to sell to all buyers or specifiers	1 2 3 4 5 6 7 8 9 10
6. Computer-based customer list	1 2 3 4 5 6 7 8 9 10
7. Use of telemarketing as support	1 2 3 4 5 6 7 8 9 10
8. Ability to sell products or systems	1 2 3 4 5 6 7 8 9 10
9. Ability to gather competitive information	1 2 3 4 5 6 7 8 9 10
10. Knowledge of our product line	1 2 3 4 5 6 7 8 9 10
11. Presale information gathering	1 2 3 4 5 6 7 8 9 10
12. Use of direct mail for end users	1 2 3 4 5 6 7 8 9 10
13. Willingness to carry inventory	1 2 3 4 5 6 7 8 9 10
14. Responsiveness to product training	1 2 3 4 5 6 7 8 9 10
15. Follow-up on lost orders	1 2 3 4 5 6 7 8 9 10
16. Ability to present proposals	1 2 3 4 5 6 7 8 9 10
17. Sales and quotation reporting	1 2 3 4 5 6 7 8 9 10
18. Territory organization and management	1 2 3 4 5 6 7 8 9 10
19. Overall communication with factory	1 2 3 4 5 6 7 8 9 10
20. Quality of sales coverage and forecasting	1 2 3 4 5 6 7 8 9 10

Total score_____

This simple performance scale is designed to give you a quick assessment of your distributor firm. If the total score is below 100, you probably have problems that will eventually lead to termination. Take action now.

Conduct periodic performance reviews. In my own experience, I have seen many sales relationships that could have been improved and other situations in which divorce could have been avoided, if either party had had an obligation to evaluate the other's performance and a method for making the evaluation. One method is to use a performance scale that rates each party in terms of agreed-upon performance criteria specific to the business.

The performance scales in Figures 7–5, 7–6, and 7–7 focus on the tasks of selling and distributing technical or engineered products. They are designed to serve as models to help you customize your own form. Rate a

FIGURE 7–6
Rep Performance Scale

Rate a rep that currently represents your company on a scale of 1 (awful) to 10 (superb)

	1	2	3	4	5	6	7	8	9	10
1. Focus on the right market niches	1	2	3	4	5	6	7	8	9	10
2. Compatibility of other product lines	1	2	3	4	5	6	7	8	9	10
3. Technical background and knowledge	1	2	3	4	5	6	7	8	9	10
4. Responsiveness to leads and account opportunities	1	2	3	4	5	6	7	8	9	10
5. Ability to sell in new markets	1	2	3	4	5	6	7	8	9	10
6. Computer-based lead and sale tracking	1	2	3	4	5	6	7	8	9	10
7. Use of telemarketing as support	1	2	3	4	5	6	7	8	9	10
8. Ability to sell systems	1	2	3	4	5	6	7	8	9	10
9. Frequency of requests for more leads	1	2	3	4	5	6	7	8	9	10
10. Knowledge of your product line	1	2	3	4	5	6	7	8	9	10
11. Presale information gathering	1	2	3	4	5	6	7	8	9	10
12. Use of direct mail for market probes	1	2	3	4	5	6	7	8	9	10
13. Provision of customer CAD drawings	1	2	3	4	5	6	7	8	9	10
14. Responsiveness to product training	1	2	3	4	5	6	7	8	9	10
15. Follow-up on lost orders	1	2	3	4	5	6	7	8	9	10
16. Ability to make proposals and give quotations	1	2	3	4	5	6	7	8	9	10
17. Sales and quotation reporting	1	2	3	4	5	6	7	8	9	10
18. Territory organization and management	1	2	3	4	5	6	7	8	9	10
19. Overall communication with factory	1	2	3	4	5	6	7	8	9	10
20. Quality of sales coverage and forecasting	1	2	3	4	5	6	7	8	9	10

Total score_____

This simple performance scale is designed to give you a quick assessment of your rep firm. If the total score is below 100, you probably have problems that will eventually lead to termination. Look into them now.

---

principal or sales organization whose performance is marginal, and then use the forms as an agenda for a meeting on how to improve.

Provide direction and leads. What is needed to make the relationship between the manufacturer and the independent rep work? "The principal investing in a marketing plan that provides the direction and necessary leads to help us in our territories," says Rich Rice, president of Catawba Packaging, a successful packaging machinery agency in Port Clinton, Ohio. Rich continues:

> We need to know what niche markets the principal is targeting, by SIC code, and we need an advertising program that targets these niches and produces a

FIGURE 7–7
Factory Performance Scale

Rate a principal (factory) that you represent, on a scale of 1 (awful) to 10 (superb)

	1	2	3	4	5	6	7	8	9	10
1. Number and quality of sales leads	1	2	3	4	5	6	7	8	9	10
2. Sales engineering support	1	2	3	4	5	6	7	8	9	10
3. Responses to fax, phone, and mail	1	2	3	4	5	6	7	8	9	10
4. Reliability of delivery promises	1	2	3	4	5	6	7	8	9	10
5. Introduction of new products	1	2	3	4	5	6	7	8	9	10
6. Sales call support in field	1	2	3	4	5	6	7	8	9	10
7. Customer service and parts support	1	2	3	4	5	6	7	8	9	10
8. Effectiveness of product training	1	2	3	4	5	6	7	8	9	10
9. Responsiveness to customer problems	1	2	3	4	5	6	7	8	9	10
10. Accuracy and responsiveness of quotes	1	2	3	4	5	6	7	8	9	10
11. Overall commitment to quality	1	2	3	4	5	6	7	8	9	10
12. Payment of commissions on time	1	2	3	4	5	6	7	8	9	10
13. Knowledge of markets	1	2	3	4	5	6	7	8	9	10
14. Assistance in defining markets	1	2	3	4	5	6	7	8	9	10
15. Direct mail assistance	1	2	3	4	5	6	7	8	9	10
16. Operator and technical manuals	1	2	3	4	5	6	7	8	9	10
17. Effectiveness of advertising	1	2	3	4	5	6	7	8	9	10
18. Trade show support	1	2	3	4	5	6	7	8	9	10
19. Sales application information	1	2	3	4	5	6	7	8	9	10
20. Usable pricing information	1	2	3	4	5	6	7	8	9	10

Total score_____

If the total score is below 100, you probably have problems that will hurt your sales effort. Take action now.

---

large number of good leads. We only have about 500 hours to devote to face-to-face calls in our large territory each year, so we need to focus our time on the best potential accounts and niches. Reps in our industry live or die on qualified leads from the principals, because new machinery projects are very hard to find, and more than half of our annual business is from new accounts.[9]

Provide timely responses. Being responsive to the independent rep's phone calls and information requests is another key to making the marriage work. When technical buyers request information in this age of fax machines and Express Mail, they expect immediate response. It is important to build an inside sales department that can respond quickly with quotations, technical information, pricing, delivery information, and answers. If these responses are lacking or slow, the factory takes the blame for lost sales opportunities. If the answer or information will take time to get, it is vital to get back to the rep and at least tell him or her when you will respond.

R. Wade Shepard, a rep from Charlotte, North Carolina, says:

> If a manufacturer wants to be the top-ranking principal in our minds, they must return our phone calls promptly, give us timely quotes, answers, etc. . . . so we can respond quickly to customers . . . [and] keep literature, technical manuals up to date so we can know the product thoroughly. . . . For a principal to be on the lowest rung of our ladder, let them simply do the opposite of the things mentioned above. They will have us angry, disappointed, and frustrated on a daily basis, and we will soon be putting our sales emphasis on pushing our other lines.[10]

Provide sales tools and information. Many factories are guilty of not spending the time to provide the technical information and materials necessary for reps to get and hold a customer's attention. Charlie Roseberry, an independent rep specializing in material handling systems, spent years in various factory sales positions before venturing into the manufacturers' rep game.

> I never realized how important it is to provide catalogs, price information, news on new products, application information, until I became a rep and got on this end of the phone. It takes five or more calls on a new account to make a sale. Buyers are extremely busy, and we reps need to find five or more reasons to get the customer to let us come back. The principals who recognize this work hard to supply us with new and prompt information about products and applications to help us make the necessary calls. Reps naturally spend more time for principals who provide this kind of support.[11]

Bulletins on new products, application reports, and information on sales successes in other markets are very important to the independent sales company. Phillips Roland, an independent rep from Somers, Connecticut, who sells instrumentation and controls, relies on principals who keep reps appraised about their future market and product development plans. He says:

> Unique new applications of principals' products in other areas of the United States and new markets and or applications that have been penetrated will allow me to enter new markets with application specific recommendations and

references. As a single-man agency, the greatest danger is myopic vision. We tend to develop a tunnel vision mentality that good competitive info and 'how to' stories from our principals can help us see the forest from the trees. Too often, principals believe we have all of the answers. We depend a great deal on their market information.[12]

Train, train, train.   Kathy Wakefield, of Pacific Air Switch Corporation, is a big proponent of technically trained independent reps. She says:

> I have always heard that reps "eat what they kill." This is a good description because independent reps are compensated in direct proportion to the results they achieve. I would stack an independent rep up against a factory salesman in our industry anytime. Reps are hard working, and deserve the same support and training you would offer a factory salesperson or any employee.[13]

An ongoing program of technical training is essential to make the marriage work. Factories should provide training on products, applications, and new developments in formal class settings as well as at the rep's home office. A good compromise is to bear all costs of training but ask the reps to pay their way to the training session.

If technical knowledge is power, factories must be tough and demanding about product training, and they must offer more security to the people who make the investment. Wakefield places a high value on technical knowledge and looks for reps that have technical educations and training in the industry. She says, "There are plenty of reps that have good technical qualifications, and it is just a matter of doing a good job of selecting the right ones for your products."[12]

Provide assurance.   Rich Rice, an independent rep, agrees that independent reps should be willing to make the training investment and take on some of the tasks normally done by factory people. But he quickly adds:

> If we are expected to become technically competent enough to handle most of the sales job ourselves, then we want some kind of assurance that this is a long-term partnership. Many principals no longer offer exclusive agreements. It is difficult for a rep firm to invest the time in training and performing many other tasks that a factory salesman would perform, when you know you could be canceled or replaced with one phone call.

FIGURE 7–8
The Do's and Don'ts of Working with Independents

Do's

✓ Do provide special compensation for new product and market development calls.

✓ Do provide ongoing technical training.

✓ Do include the primary points of sales coverage in the contract and agree to an annual factory/rep performance evaluation.

✓ Do provide ongoing information like new product bulletins, application reports, and information on sales successes.

✓ Do make sure all factory sales and support people walk in reps' shoes by making the difficult market and product development sales calls.

✓ Do give independent reps the same level of respect and support you would your own employees.

Don'ts

✓ Don't fail to pay commissions when you have collected from the customer.

✓ Don't fail to provide enough leads to help reps probe market niches for projects.

✓ Don't expect reps to develop a target marketing plan for you.

✓ Don't fail to return phone calls or respond to written requests.

✓ Don't fail to make customer delivery commitments.

✓ Don't delay in responding to customer service problems.

Walk a mile in the rep's shoes. People inside a corporation who never travel with independent sales reps are insulated from the problems of the rep. They don't realize how much hard work and how many calls it takes to develop credibility, much less to get an order. "Many people at the factory think that orders simply come in the mail," says Jack McNally, dealer sales manager for Columbia Steel Casting Company.

> They never really have to go out in the field and experience what reps and dealer salespeople really have to do to get an order. Everybody gets in the act when an order is being processed, but few people understand that developing the account took years of sales calls, phone calls, letters, quotations, and boring hours traveling in the car just to get a chance. No matter how you might explain it, people really can't fairly assess the work of independent salespeople unless they have been on the firing line and have really stood in their shoes.[14]

Even factory sales managers don't know what it is like to stand in a rep's shoes. They show little respect for the independent rep's work schedule, according to Rich Rice. Rice has many stories about factory sales managers who want to come into the territory and make sales calls with one-day notice.

They act like we don't have anything to do or that we can simply alter our plans to fit them. When it happens, it always gives the sales manager the wrong impression of the independent reps' tasks. We pick them up at a fancy hotel and escort them to the projects that we have worked on for years, that are about to close. They don't have to carry the conversation, are treated like royalty, and then go away with the order, saying to themselves, "This sales game is pretty easy."

Treat them like employees.   Independent reps and distributors are business people just as you are, and they deserve a lot of credit for all the work it takes to accomplish the elusive requirements of sales coverage. If you want good reps, treat them like members of your team, and give them the same respect you would an employee. It's good to have high expectations, but make sure that you provide the support your reps and distributors need to achieve them. Don't commit the sins outlined in Figure 7–8.

SHOULD YOU CHANGE CHANNELS?

Now that you have looked at many distribution channel strategies, examples of what other SMMs did, and the major issues involved in selecting channels, the question is: Do you need to change your current channels? One thing is certain: If you decide to become a niche marketer, you are going to have to develop a channel strategy that supports your niche marketing plan. This means finding a simple way to examine the sales tasks required to reach each customer niche.

At the risk of oversimplifying a fairly complicated marketing strategy, here are five steps to help you evaluate various channel possibilities:

Step 1.   Using the techniques and examples shown in this chapter, develop a list of niches or accounts. Don't spend a lot of time on this step. Just group customers by account size, industry, product, or whatever results in a simple grouping.

Step 2.   Assess the tasks required to sell to each of these niches or customer groups. You can break the tasks down into very specific sales steps, or simply list the general tasks—for example, qualifying prospects, gathering presale information, closing a sale, and providing postsale services. The question is: Can the channel efficiently handle all tasks for all customers?

Step 3.   Assess the costs of selling to all niches and customers. The previous information on using cost of sale, the sell price rule, and territory breakeven formulas may come in handy as you evaluate sales costs.

Step 4.   Critically assess your current sales organization in terms of capabilities, interest, and time. Use the performance scales shown in Figures 7–5 and 7–6 to help highlight obvious areas of strengths and weaknesses. Does the organization have the time to do a good job on all accounts? Is it cost-effective to call on all accounts? Do salespeople have the talents and interest to focus on specific niches?

Step 5.   Decide who the primary targets are (the prospects that must be covered) and determine where the voids in coverage are. Segregate the small accounts, geographically scattered accounts, and special niches that are not getting sales coverage, or are getting sales calls that are not cost-justifiable.

If the current sales force doesn't have the time, capability, or interest to cover all the accounts and you have established the coverage voids, this little exercise will be the first step toward establishing a more efficient and more effective channel strategy.

*   *   *   *   *

Now that I have discussed how to optimize distribution channels, it's time to focus on developing a low-cost, high-impact niche advertising strategy—the subject of Chapter 8.

KEY POINT

Traditional channels of distribution are no longer adequate to serve the needs of a wide variety of customers and market niches. SMMs should consider exploring new channels, to reduce selling costs and improve sales coverage.

SUGGESTED ACTION

Send a copy of the performance scale shown in Figure 7–7 to all your direct salespeople, agents, and/or distributors, to get a quick assessment of how well you are supporting them. Have the sales manager fill out a performance scale (Figure 7–5 or Figure 7–6) on each of the salespeople and pinpoint problems common to all of them. This will give you a report card on your channel relationships, with a list of specific areas that need improvement.

NOTES

1. Copyright © 1990 by the President and Fellows of Harvard College; all rights reserved. Reprinted by permission of *Harvard Business Review* by Rowland T Moriarty and Ursula Moran, "Managing Hybrid Marketing Systems," November–December 1990, p. 146.

2. Harold J Novick, "Reps Beat the Slow-Growth Catch 22," *Business Marketing,* Crains Communications, Inc., December 1987, pp. 65–67.

3. Personal interview with the author, March 1993.

4. Bob Stone, *Successful Direct Marketing Methods* (Chicago: Crain Books, 1984), p. 1.

5. Excerpts from telephone interview with Chuck Martin and copy of Chuck Martin's original telemarketing business plan.

6. Quotes from telephone interview and Chuck Martin's original telemarketing business plan.

7. "Investments in Marketing Costs as a Percent of Sales Vary Across Industries," *LAP Report 8015.6* (New York: McGraw-Hill, 1984).

8. Stanley R Rich and David Gumpert, *Business Plans that Win $* (New York: Harper and Row, 1987), p. 91.

9. From phone interview with Richard Rice, April and May 1993.

10. "Agents Tell What They Like about Their Favorite Principals," *Agency Sales Magazine,* March 1991, pp. 57–59. Reprinted from Agency Sales Magazine, Copyright © 1991, Manufacturers' Agents National Association, 23016 Mill Creek Road, P.O. Box 3467, Laguna Hills, California 92654-3467, (714) 859-4040, fax (714) 855-2973. All rights reserved. Reproduction without permission is strictly prohibited.

11. Personal interview with Charlie Roseberry, March 1993.

12. "Agents Report on the Kind Of Marketing Information They Find Most Helpful from Their Principals," *Agency Sales Magazine,* August 1992, p. 15. Reprinted from *Agency Sales Magazine,* Copyright © 1992, Manufacturers' Agents National Association, 23016 Mill Creek Road, P.O. Box 3467, Laguna Hills, California 92654-3467, (714) 859-4040; fax

13. Personal interviews with the author, April and May 1993.

14. Personal interview with Jack McNally, May and June 1993.

Chapter Eight

Niche Advertising Strategies
*How to Get More Bang for the
Advertising Buck*

DO YOU NEED TO ADVERTISE?

Before we discuss how to develop an effective—and cost-effective—advertising program, let's determine whether you need one. Contrary to what media salespeople might tell you, not all companies have to advertise. Whether or not advertising is necessary depends on the type of product you are selling, the type of accounts you are selling to, and whether or not your company is introducing a new product or developing a new market.

Standardized or Specialized Products,
Customers Known

If your product is standardized (versus customized), and if all your customers are known, you may not need to advertise. For example, a manufacturer that offers a catalog of standard fittings, which are sold to a limited number of paper mills through a manufacturer's rep, probably doesn't need much advertising support.

If your product is specialized, it still may not be necessary to do much advertising if you know all your customers. For example, a manufacturer of built-to-spec (bid) industrial air switches, which are marketed to the 200 known utility companies in the United States by independent reps who know all the buyers and engineers in every utility, doesn't need to advertise.

Standardized or Specialized Products, Customers Unknown

Many SMMs develop innovative products but are not sure of all the prospects or applications for them. A specialized product like a custom-built production machine may be sold for a variety of applications, requiring slight modifications, and advertising is the most practical way of finding these applications.

Engineered Capital Products or Funded Projects

A manufacturer of custom-built automation equipment that is used on the production lines of large manufacturing companies must first find a capital project in a territory that may have thousands of plants or a company with thousands of employees. The buyers are unknown, and salespeople cannot personally call on every plant in their territory. In this situation, advertising is an absolute necessity. It takes a combination of trade journal advertising, an aggressive publicity campaign, and direct mail to targeted niches to produce enough inquiries to probe for projects.

BOTTOM-LINE ADVERTISING

If you decide it's worth your while to advertise, make sure you get the most for your advertising dollars. Many advertising professionals like to describe advertising as a presell tool. They talk in terms of the number of prospects reached or the impressions their ads make on readers. The owners of SMMs may not understand all the presell objectives, but they do understand orders. If they can't see a link between the two, they may cut the advertising budget.

The owners and managers of SMMs are usually bottom-line-oriented. They identify more with the tactics for securing orders than with the vagaries involved in generation of advertising inquiries. No manager or owner of a small or midsized manufacturing company is going to continue to spend much money on advertising and promotion unless it can be justified. SMMs cannot afford to waste their limited resources. The bottom-line justification for advertising is sales. The message for SMMs is that everyone involved with designing or approving advertising expenditures should spend more creative energy on linking advertising to sales.

ADVERTISING ON A SHOESTRING BUDGET

Some midsize manufacturers with advertising departments and adequate budgets may need little help in improving the efficiency and effectiveness of their advertising programs. Small manufacturing companies, however, with budgets to match, must find very efficient ways to reach the right prospects and markets and to get the most out of every ad dollar. They simply don't have the money to spend on a multilevel advertising program.

Luckily, it doesn't take a lot of money to stimulate your target customers if you know who they are and if you can focus your limited resources on them. Three examples that show how this can be done are described below.

A Low-Cost Product Introduction to a New Market

When a company's market niche and prospects are not precisely defined, which is the case for many new products, the company is forced to test the waters by running ads or publicity releases in a wide variety of trade journals, in order to generate a lot of initial inquiries. With this first round of inquiries in hand, the company can narrow its focus and eventually refine its market niche by progressive qualifying of prospects and measurement of responses from various media.

An example of a very successful campaign accomplished on a tight budget is OrCAD Systems' introduction of a new CAE (computer-aipen engineering) software product in 1986. The company had been started with bootstrap financing from the owners and relatives. There was little money available for advertising and promotion, and the program had to be financed and sustained from sales revenues.

The company founder began by advertising and running publicity in a variety of electronics industry trade journals to help define the niche. They took eight steps to define the market:

Step 1. They ran ⅑-page ads (some black-and-white, some two-color) in five electronics trade journals. They combined this with an aggressive, low-cost publicity campaign that involved sending out press releases and other new product information to a variety of trade journals. These combined efforts yielded 12,000 leads in the first year of the company's operation.

Step 2.   They segmented the inquiries and sent lead fulfillment packages to all prospects. Each lead fulfillment package included a free product demo disk.

Step 3.   Basic information (name, company name and address, and date of inquiry) about those prequalified by phone was loaded into a computer database so that the prospects could be profiled and tracked.

Step 4.   The department members followed up with phone calls to a sample of prospects to whom the lead fulfillment packages had been sent. The prospects were asked why they would buy or not buy, and the department members offered to assist the prospects in ordering the product.

Step 5.   Based on the inquiries they received, the department modified its advertising message and ad layout to make them more attractive to qualified prospects.

Step 6.   The department measured the effectiveness of its ad campaigns by comparing orders to original inquiries, using the computer database.

Step 7.   The department members evaluated the effectiveness of the media and the message by counting the inquiries generated by each magazine and advertisement.

Step 8.   They used the response to publicity releases to pretest the readership for an advertisement. Many publicity inquirers called in by phone, which allowed the company to profile the prospects and find out whether an ad in the particular magazine would be worthwhile.

OrCAD had to start with a general approach in order to generate enough inquiries to begin the process of finding its target customers. Or-CAD's low-cost publicity/fractional ad program worked very well and as sales improved, the company increased the size and frequency of its advertising program. Using this approach, the company grew from sales of 45 units to more than 75,000 units in less than four years, proving that it doesn't take a big budget to reach targeted customers if you continuously analyze prospects and fine-tune your advertising messages.

AIM FOR THE TARGET

A shotgun advertising campaign invites inquiries from anyone, rather than appealing to specific market niches or prospects. This approach can be effective in reaching buyers, but it will also attract many inquiries from people who cannot buy or have no real interest, wasting precious advertising dollars.

This is a particularly bad problem for independent reps who depend solely on factory-generated leads to find prospects and projects. They will often lose interest if they have to plow through hundreds of inquiries from people who are not qualified prospects.

The quality of leads can be immediately improved by targeting advertising promotions and advertising messages to the customer groups identified in the market assessment (see Chapter 5). There are three ways to accomplish this, as follows:

Target the right publications. Target your market with a trade publication that reaches this group of prospective customers. Ask editors of trade journals whether their journals would be appropriate places to advertise your product. If you're not convinced by what an editor tells you, read the journal for six months and see what products are advertised and what kinds of articles are published. This will give you a feel for whether or not the magazine is appropriate for your product.

Target the message to the buyer. Make sure you tailor your message to your niches. For example, Marvin Windows of Warroad, Minnesota, manufactures windows for building supply dealers, remodelers, architects, and commercial building owners. The company has developed a different type of ad for each market niche.

A dealer ad, for example, explains that dealers can cut their inventory costs by using Marvin's products because the windows are all built to order. The ad shows an empty warehouse and the headline, "Quite frankly, we are more interested in the space between your ears."

An ad for remodelers features ease of installation by showing a photo of a window which fits the opening in a building exactly, next to a photo of a competitor's window, which does not. The headline message is, "As you can see, there's a sizable gap between Marvin's replacement windows and the others."

An ad targeted to builders shows a picture of a small standard window and a large circular, custom window made by Marvin, with the message

"We make windows for imaginations that have no limit." Under the stock window, the message continues: "And budgets that do."[1]

Each of Marvin's ads is tailored to the problems and interests of a particular customer group, and each is run in trade journals that are popular with the specific group. This is an efficient way to reach the right customers and to make the most of scarce advertising dollars.

Use direct mail to reach carefully profiled niches. Direct mail can work no matter how small your company or how tight your budget. For example, I worked with an independent rep firm, which sells packaging machinery, to develop a campaign to generate inquiries because the principals did not have a good advertising program. The rep firm had tried direct mail in the past, but the results were disappointing.

The mailer they had sent was a newsletter that featured their principals' new products. The mailer had cost $5,600, had taken two to three months to produce, and had generated very few inquiries and no sales.

Because of the firm's budget and experience limitations, we developed a program based on the following objectives:

1. *Low cost per lead.* Our objective was to get the cost of each inquiry down from $200 to less than $40.

2. *Increase the frequency of mailings.* I determined that finding projects in the firm's large territory would require at least six direct mailers at a minimum frequency of three times.

3. *Simplify the program.* Because nobody in the firm had any training in advertising, I knew that the writing, layout, and production would have to be very simple, or the program would die.

4. *Target to SIC market niches.* Each mailer was focused on a market niche defined by SIC codes, with prospects and customers that had been phone-quaiified for address changes.

5. *Keep the message simple.* The message was directed at a specific user and was designed to show in graphic form a simple problem from the buyer's perspective, with the product shown as a solution.

6. *Make it easy to respond.* We included the firm's phone and fax numbers in large print right on the mailer and asked the customers and prospects to fax the mailer back to the firm.

This simple direct mail program produced tremendous results almost immediately. The first mailer (shown in Figure 8–1) went to 2,161 addresses and cost a total of $531, including postage. It produced 20

FIGURE 8–1
A Simple Mailer

REPLACE MANUAL STACKING

SOLUTION:

FL–100 Lowest cost automatic palletizer in the U.S. today!

Let Catawba experts lay out a system that fits your space and budget.

THE PROBLEM:

✓ LOW SPEED LINES

✓ INJURIES

✓ OUT OF SQUARE PALLET LOADS

✓ SEASONAL STACKING

✓ INCREASING LABOR COSTS

TELL US YOUR NEEDS:

Products _____

Line speed (cpm) _____

No. pallet patterns _____

Name _____

Title _____

Company _____

Address _____

City/State/Zip _____

Phone _____

Call (419) 797-2175

CAN'T WAIT? FAX
419-797-2387

Source: Designed by the authors for Catawba Packaging, Inc., Port Clinton, Ohio, January 1993.

inquiries at a cost of $27 per inquiry and resulted in 10 qualified projects requiring quotations. The firm found that the mailers were easy to produce, and followed up with six more mailers, which focused on different customer groups and used different messages.

Ten Tips for Boosting Response

Following are 10 low-cost ways to improve the quantity and quality of direct mail inquiries:

1. Offer free information, such as a catalog and/or an application sheet.
2. Offer free services, such as consultation about a project, a "walk-through" review of the customer's facility and equipment, or a report that summarizes the cost savings and/or other benefits of using your product.
3. Provide useful information. Include a planning guide, a selection chart, or installation tips. Use terms that imply value—for example, use "product guide" instead of "catalog," or "planning kit" instead of "sales brochure." Develop headlines that stress user benefits.
4. Install a toll-free 800 number if you don't already have one, and show the number prominently in all your ads.
5. Make sure that trade magazines list a reader service number in all your ads.
6. To boost response by 25 to 100 percent, include a discount coupon in your ad.
7. Use a "fractional ad"—one that includes a name-and-address card readers can clip and return. Make sure the end of the ad copy asks readers to return the card. Better yet, ask readers to attach a business card and send it to you. This will produce a higher response because it's easier for the reader.
8. Include self-addressed, postage-paid reply cards with all literature kits and prospect information.
9. Offer multiple response options, such as "Please have a salesperson call," "Send free planning kit," and "I'd like to see a demonstration."
10. Use graphics in the ad—for example, an arrow pointing to an important number, or a shadow box that highlights vital information. Also, put a photo or drawing of the product on the envelope.

Here are a few more general tips to keep in mind as you develop your advertising campaign:

Keep it simple.   Don't get hung up on layout perfection, persuasive copy, or even typos. I have seen too many people become so preoccupied with the creative side of developing ads that the ad design itself, rather than the generation of inquiries that lead to sales, becomes the goal. One award-winning mailer a year that produces 100 leads doesn't compare to 10 simple mailers that produce 1,000 leads and sales. I know it is advertising heresy to say this, but everyone in the process of developing ads must be constantly reminded that the objective is not to make art, but to get orders.

Fax it.   Fax messages always get read before other mail. Sometimes it is a good idea to use the fax as a rapid response to a hot inquiry. Also, put your fax number in your ad or direct mail message. Inquirers find it very easy to write their names and addresses on an ad or a coupon and send it back to you on the fax machine.

Use niche messages.   As the Marvin Windows example makes clear, one way to focus your advertising on the right reader is via the message. Your message can help you to prequalify prospects by telling them who should buy. The direct mail piece shown in Figure 8–1 is another good example of this.

Use 800 numbers.   Readers prefer to call back on your nickel when they are interested. They know that if they fill out a bingo card, they may have to wait for weeks to get the information they need. Using 800 numbers allows you to qualify prospects early in the sales process and makes it easier for them to buy.

Invest in telephone qualification of inquiries.   Unless your cost for face-to-face sales calls is low, don't allow field reps to qualify all inquiries. Field reps don't like paperwork or wading through all the non-buyers who inquire. Providing them with large numbers of unqualified inquiries only confirms their suspicions that the ad program is no good. Give this job to a full-time (low-cost) inside person, or hire a service to qualify leads.

Respond fast.   Have you ever responded to a trade journal ad and then waited weeks for the information? Chances are that you either lost interest in the information altogether or found an alternative solution or product. Don't spend a lot of money on generating inquiries and then lose the sales leads by responding slowly.

Fast responses lead to more sales. With fax machines, modems, and overnight mail services, buyers today expect fast responses. Make quick response a top priority. Whoever reaches the prospect first with the right information is going to have the upper hand.

Send a fulfillment package within 24 hours of receiving an inquiry. If for some reason you cannot do this internally, let an outside service do it for you.

The key to fast fulfillment is preparation. Make sure you have fulfillment packages prepared for each ad or publicity release before the ads appear. Figure out what literature, reply cards, demo disks, letters and envelopes will be needed to reply to inquiries, and get them ready ahead of time. I know this sounds obvious, but interested inquirers often go begging, and this is one reason ad campaigns don't work.

Consider sending less expensive data sheets to inquirers who cannot buy (students, professors, etc.). Send the expensive packet of materials only to people who can be identified as having buying power.

Include a cover letter.   Cover letters are important because the secretary or whoever opens the mail may throw the envelope away, and the inquirer may not remember inquiring. Your cover letter should:

1. Thank the prospect for inquiring.
2. Explain benefits or savings.
3. Sell the product or service.
4. Make an offer.
5. Ask the prospect to take action.

Figure 8–2 shows an example of an effective cover letter.

TRACKING ADVERTISING RESULTS

What little money SMMs do spend on advertising, they often spend reluctantly. Many owners and managers of SMMs suspect that a large part of their advertising budget is wasted. Sometimes they're right. If they

FIGURE 8–2
Sample Cover Letter

Dear Sir or Madam:

Thank you for your interest in the FABTEK Data Collection Systems. Whether you need quality or increased productivity, a FABTEK system will deliver substantial savings.

- A paper manufacturer cut scrap by 55 percent using a FABTEK system.
- A machine shop saved 20 minutes per hour by replacing handwritten methods with direct recording of measurements into a FABTEK.
- A peripherals manufacturer used to take five days to collect attribute data. A FABTEK system has cut it to eight hours.
- A machinery manufacturer is saving $50,000 per year using a $5,000 FABTEK system.

FABTEK systems are used for attribute auditing, controlling package weights, fit and finish inspection, measurement verification, machine tool capability studies, torque auditing, and a wide range of other applications.

Ford Motor Company has more than 1,000 systems in use. Caterpillar, Monsanto, GM, IBM, Kodak, Rockwell—all use FABTEK systems.

A good FABTEK system pays for itself in less than three months. In fact, if you have a good application, and give us half your monthly savings for two years, we will give you a FABTEK system free.

Please call us for a free application survey.

Sincerely,

---

are not spending their money wisely—for example, if direct mail is sent to the wrong prospects or if their ads carry the wrong message—they may indeed be wasting their money. However, unless they measure the results of their advertising and promotion campaigns, they have no way of knowing.

Measurement involves such things as:

- Sorting all inquiries by ad and media source, and determining the cost per inquiry.
- Keeping an ongoing database of inquiries and matching them to orders to justify ad costs with sales dollars.
- Keeping track of the percentage of qualified leads from the total number of inquiries.

- Conducting periodic "did you buy" phone surveys (discussed below) to determine the percentage of prospects who purchased.

Unfortunately, few SMMs bother to measure the results of their advertising efforts. It's not uncommon for an SMM to spend tens of thousands of dollars on field sales and advertising programs, yet to invest little time and money on measurement of results. The company may take out ads in several trade journals, mail pieces directly to thousands of prospects, develop and distribute four-color brochures, send out press releases, and have no idea what the return on the investment is. Unless the managers trace sales to specific advertising efforts, they have no way of knowing what worked and what didn't.

True, it's sometimes hard to track sales back to leads. For example, if a product is sold through a distributor, the distributor's customers will have to be tracked. If there are thousands of inquiries and the company's order system is separate from its inquiry system, it will be difficult to match sales to leads. Such problems make tracking difficult, but these are not the main reasons for SMMs' failure to measure advertising results.

In my experience, the biggest reason SMMs don't track inquiries to orders is simply that no one wants to bother doing this tedious chore. It's easier, and much more fun, to run ads than to measure their results.

Simple Tracking Techniques

Tracking inquiries to sales is a lot easier than you might think. Resourceful SMMs have developed a number of simple and effective tracking techniques. The two most popular methods are mail and telephone surveys.

Mail surveys.   The simplest way to track the results of an ad campaign is to include a postage-paid "bounce back card" with all the fulfillment packages you send out. However, unless you mail the cards to a representative sample of qualified prospects rather than to any and every person who inquires, your results will probably be poor. Because the sample isn't representative of those who will buy your products, the information won't help you much. However, this technique is better than doing nothing.

A better method is to send a follow-up survey only to qualified prospects. For example, a technology company advertised its products in trade journals, on product cards, in news releases, at trade shows, and

FIGURE 8–3
Tracing Advertising through to Sales

Total cost of advertising program	$35,000
Number of raw inquiries produced	3,305
Number of inquiries qualified by phone or mail	1,032
Cost per qualified inquiry	$34 each
Number of qualified leads who responded	389
Number of qualified leads who purchased	126
Total sales from these leads	$1.25 million
Average sale value	$10,000
Average return per ad dollar	$35.71

through direct mail. The campaign cost $35,000 and yielded 3,305 inquiries.

Out of these inquiries, the company sent a follow-up direct mail piece to 1,032 qualified leads. The piece was a simple, personalized one-page letter that included six questions on whether or not the prospect bought or intended to buy, and why or why not.

Of the 1,032 prospects who were sent the mailer, 389 responded within six weeks—a 38 percent response rate. Of these, 126 ended up buying a product from the company. The direct mail program, including follow-up, generated $1.25 million in sales. For every dollar spent on advertising, the company got back $35.71 in sales.[2] Figure 8–3 shows the detailed results of the campaign.

Telephone surveys.   Telephone surveys can greatly increase the effectiveness of advertising campaigns. A 1993 study by Cahners found that 79 percent of inquiries receive some kind of follow-up information in the mail (such as a bounce back card), but only 11 percent receive a telephone call.[3] By not following up with a phone call, SMMs are neglecting an easy method of determining the effectiveness of their advertising. They may also be losing out on sales: several publisher surveys, including Cahners', have repeatedly shown that many people who inquire about a company's products end up buying from a competitor because nobody bothered to follow up on the lead.

Lost leads are a gold mine of immediate sales potential that can be exploited by SMMs. All that is required is a better follow-up system—including follow-up telephone calls made to inquirers.

Consider conducting a telephone survey six months after an ad appears. Select 100 to 150 qualified leads and call every one of them. The objective is to determine whether the prospects purchased, how well the leads were followed up, what future sales potential still exists, and "what a qualified lead should be for future projects."[4] Figure 8–4 is a sample buyer survey that you can use for the experiment. If you don't have time, hire an outside firm to do it.

You may be surprised at how many qualified buyers your advertising generated and even more surprised at how many of these buyers purchased competitors' products. This information can be used to justify starting a formal inquiry follow-up system, or perhaps to refocus your advertising program or change the message in your advertisements.

If you generate thousands of inquiries over a long period of time, the job of tracking them usually requires a computer database. If you are not comfortable with computers and databases, consider hiring an inquiry handling service to build and manage the database and conduct buyer surveys for you. (These services are listed in the Yellow Pages under a heading such as "Sales Inquiry Services.") It will cost you $2,000 or so to have a professional service track your leads using their own software and database management system. This cost typically includes 30 hours of telemarketing, tabulation, and an executive summary of the study results, according to Inquiry Handling Service, which is based in San Fernando, California.

HOW TO GENERATE FREE PUBLICITY

Much publicity—including press releases, new product releases, and articles and notices in trade publications—is virtually free to the SMM that knows how to generate it. Because of this, publicity should be at the top of the marketing lists of all manufacturing firms with limited budgets.

Here are some helpful hints for generating free publicity:

- *Target industry publications.* Get a complete list of all magazines and publications that cover your market niches. If you can't identify your market niches, begin with all publications that are targeted to your industry, then gradually narrow the focus by analyzing who responds. Make sure that every publication on the list actually offers new product and publicity releases. Directories such as *Bacon's Publicity Checker* (published by Bacon's Publishing, Chicago) can help you find which magazines do.

FIGURE 8–4
Inquiry Handling Service, Inc.
Sample "Did-You-Buy" Survey

NAME _____ TITLE_____

COMPANY _____

DEPT./MAIL STOP _____

ADDRESS/P.O. BOX _____

CITY _____ STATE _____ ZIP _____

DAYTIME PHONE (_____) _____ EXT _____

Within the past few months, you inquired about a product. We are conducting this market research project to help find out what happened as a result of inquiries such as yours. Will you please take a moment to answer a few questions?

1. Do you recall inquiring about the product? ☐ Yes ☐ No
2. Did you receive the information that you requested? ☐ Yes ☐ No
3. Were you contacted by a ☐ Representative   ☐ Distributor
                            ☐ Regional manager   ☐ Not contacted
4. Did you contact someone after receiving the information?   ☐ Yes ☐ No
5. Did you make inquiries to other manufacturers about similar products? ☐ Yes ☐ No
   If yes, which other manufacturers? _____
6. Since making an inquiry, have you purchased any products?   ☐ Yes ☐ No
   If yes, from whom have you purchased?_____
   Why? _____
7. Are you still in the market for the product?   ☐ Yes ☐ No
   If yes, when do you plan to buy?
      ☐ Within 3 months   ☐ 7–12 months
      ☐ 3–6 months   ☐ Longer than 12 months
8. How many do you expect to purchase? ☐ Less than 5 ☐ 6–10 ☐ More than 10
9. If you haven't yet purchased since receiving the information, what manufacturers or models are you considering? _____
   _____
10. What is your intended application? _____
11. Would you like to have a representative contact you?   ☐ Yes   ☐ No
    If yes, best time: _____AM   _____PM

CORPORATE HEADQUARTERS   NORTHERN CALIFORNIA SALES OFFICE
200 Parkside Drive   2010 Crow Canyon Place, Suite 110
San Fernando, CA 91340-3092   San Ramon, CA 94583-1300
(818) 365-8131   Fax (818) 365-1876   (510) 277-0783   Fax (510) 277-1282

Source: IHS Tele-Survey Market Research Service, Inquiry Handling Service, Inc., San Fernando, CA, 1993.

- *Get to know editors.*   Magazine editors have to choose publicity ideas from a stack of hundreds of possibilities. You need to form a relationship with the editors of trade publications that serve your market niches and provide some reasons why they should put your publicity into their magazine. Call them on the phone and introduce yourself and your company. Buy them lunch when you're in their area, or when they're in yours.

- *Write your own releases.*   You don't have to hire an ad agency to write press releases. Magazines give you only a tiny bit of space anyway, and you don't need to write very much. Look at other people's releases, and develop a standard format that you can use every time. You can find plenty of examples in new product or publicity sections of trade journals.

- *Target your message.*   Just as you would do in your ads, make the headline or at least part of the message of your press release focus on the specific market niche or customer you are targeting. For example, a single-board computer manufacturer used the abbreviation "OEM" in all publicity and advertising messages because the company was trying to establish OEM agreements with specialized manufacturers in the electronics industry.

  Make sure that you describe some user benefits for the target customer. Examples are: "Energy costs are reduced because steam production is cut back" and "Prevents product blowout during transit."

- Take photos.   If you build customized or engineered products, set up a method for photographing every product before it is shipped. The photos can be sent out when you mail press releases. (It's a good idea to have them for service problems and product liability suits, anyway.)

- *Make it a habit.*   An ongoing program of monthly press releases will produce considerable inquiries at a low cost per inquiry. A line extension, a new model, a new brochure, or even an accessory can be news to the right prospect or customer. However, most SMMs do not plan for a consistent publicity program. Specifically, they do not take photographs on a regular basis, even though photos are needed to produce a steady stream of effective press releases. If you are not taking photographs and producing press releases on a regular basis, get into the habit.

- *Measure results.*   Keep track of all the press releases you send. Have someone track all inquiries generated per magazine, and keep records of both the quantity and the quality of inquiries. Favor magazines that habitually run your releases—particularly if they are magazines that your buyers read.

*   *   *   *   *

This chapter has shown how SMMs can improve sales results by focusing their advertising messages, taking advantage of free publicity, getting the most out of the leads that are generated, and measuring advertising results. Chapter 9 will explain how to set sales priorities and manage a sales territory effectively, after your advertising strategy is in place.

KEY POINT

You should make every effort to trace inquiries to sales, to measure the cost per lead, to determine which advertising messages work best, and to find out how many qualified prospects purchase your product, by conducting periodic buyer surveys.

SUGGESTED ACTION

Assign someone on your staff, or a consultant, the task of doing a manual comparison of inquiries and orders for the last two years and conducting a survey of 100 qualified prospects. If inquiries can't be tracked to sales, or if you find that few inquirers say they purchased your product, reexamine your advertising program to make sure that it is focused on the right market niches and that you are delivering the right message.

NOTES

1. "Talking Customer Talk," *Business Marketing,* October 1989, p. 52.
2. Ronald M Gwynn, "Tracking Advertising through to Sales," *Business Marketing,* February 1985, pp. 90–98.
3. "Are Inquiries Contacted by Companies After Requesting Information through a Reader Service Card?" in *Cahners Advertising Research Report 210.5B* (Newton, MA: Cahners Publishing Company, June 1993).
4. "Program Objectives," IHS Tele-Survey Market Research Service, Inquiry Handling Service, Inc., San Fernando, CA, 1993.

Chapter Nine

Developing an Effective Sales Strategy

In Chapter 1, I noted that the majority of small and midsize manufacturers tend to think that more sales will solve all their production, cash flow, service and other problems. This puts enormous pressure on the sales department to produce a continuous stream of new orders. This, in turn, makes salespeople receptive to what I call *magic-key* approaches to sales.

A wide variety of popular books and seminars, with titles like *How to Double Your Sales in One Week* and *12 Secrets for Improving Your Closing Ratio,* sell the idea that there is a magic key the salesperson can use to touch the buyer's "hot buttons" and shorten the selling process.

The magic-key approach might work for inexpensive, standardized products with which one-on-one personal selling techniques can be used and the cost of a sales call is relatively low. However, more often than not, business selling involves large corporate buyers and expensive, highly technical, customized products on the right-hand side of the product range (see Chapter 6). The sales cycle for these products can span several years. In a bid project, the customer is virtually impossible to identify unless a RFQ is submitted or until a project is funded.

More sophisticated, better-educated buyers demand a lot of documentation and technical communication. Buying decisions aren't made by a single person over a cup of coffee but by a decision-making unit (DMU), a team of people who evaluate the product and decide whether to buy it. This customer team is assembled on a one-time basis, and every major project thus represents a new customer. Customers issue lengthy bids or RFQs that must be answered with lengthy proposals. Finally, the cost of a technical sales call is often very high, and salespeople must spend many hours to develop new accounts. These complex sales require a far different set of skills from the personal selling techniques taught in most sales seminars.

This chapter will focus on the difficulties of selling complex technical products. The first part of the chapter will highlight the challenges of selling to large companies, using the example of Buzz Bigby, a typical manufacturer's rep. The second part of the chapter will outline strategies SMMs can use to make the most of their limited selling time and budgets, focusing on the example of Industrial Power, Inc., a small manufacturer of hydraulics accessories.

THE SAGA OF BUZZ BIGBY

Selling complex technical products to large companies requires a different breed of salesperson from the traditional rep of the past, who got by on personality and guile. Like Buzz Bigby.

Buzz is a manufacturer's rep who sells machinery for five different companies. An imposing figure with straight teeth and a crooked smile, Buzz is the classic extrovert. He gets along well with everybody. He works long hours and can make more calls in a day than most people can in a week.

But Buzz has fallen on hard times in recent years. Last year he lost the ABC line after being a rep for 15 years. He was told that his territory coverage had slipped, and he just wasn't making any headway in selling to the large companies in his territory. He has also been getting a lot of flack from other principals about his unwillingness to fill out quotation and sales coverage reports. To add to his problems, one of Buzz's best principals recently decided to "sell direct" to a large multinational company, because the corporate engineering group complained that Buzz wasn't able to answer their technical questions.

The Five Challenges of Selling to Large Corporations

After more than 20 years in the business, Buzz suddenly feels like a stranger in a strange land. He's finding that the sales approaches that were successful in the past don't work on the younger, more technically oriented buyers to whom he must sell today. In short, Buzz has come face to face with the harsh realities of selling to large corporations in the 1990s, and he's having a difficult time adjusting to them.

Challenge #1: Individuals don't buy products; DMUs do.
Buzz sells technical products and systems. He is accustomed to selling

products to small plants. Because of the many mergers and acquisitions that have taken place over the last few years, there are fewer small plants and more large corporate buyers in his territory today.

Instead of selling one-on-one to the company owner or manager, Buzz must now convince a whole group of corporate representatives—a *decision-making unit*—to buy his products. He must contend with engineers who ask difficult technical questions, purchasing agents who present complex RFQs, and occasional meetings at which people from all over the company ask questions. Buzz is intimidated by these younger buyers, who flaunt their class rings and seem to be comfortable in meetings that simply lead to more meetings. He often complains, "I am a salesman, not a meeting coordinator."

Just as individual market niches require unique strategies, large companies demand special selling techniques, support, and products. Figure 9–1 shows the differences between selling to small plants and selling to giant corporations, in terms of who makes the buying decision, the format of sales calls, the amount of paperwork required to close the sale, selling techniques, communication style, and the extent of technical personnel the sales rep must deal with.

Large accounts represent special problems for independent salespeople, because they can consume large chunks of time. This is a serious problem for independent reps and distributors, because they have to achieve minimum coverage on many customers for several different principals.

It is vital that salespeople have the skills and credibility to handle the accounts assigned them. If they can't do the job or if they continuously need help, the manufacturer should consider either (1) offering additional training and/or support or (2) changing its representation. For an Ohio rep firm that sells to the food industry, the solution was to assign sales coverage by account rather than by geographic territory.

It's tough for a salesperson who is accustomed to selling in a small-company environment to make the transition to a large corporation. The Ohio rep firm got around this problem by dividing up its accounts among different salespeople, according to their selling abilities.

Challenge #2:   Technical sales require technical knowledge.
Standardized, off-the-shelf products can be learned quickly by the professional salesperson. But many business products require that salespeople have considerable technical knowledge and a big investment in training.

FIGURE 9–1
The Large-Customer Dilemma

Needs	Small Plant	Large Plant	Multiunit Division
Decision maker	Owner	Specifiers or buyers	DMU committees
Sales calls	Drop-ins	Appointments	Large meetings
Paperwork	Minimal	Specs and bids	Complicated RFQs
Selling	Personal	Some factory assistance	Executive team
Communication	Verbal	Written	Extensive documentation
Engineering	Rough sketch	Formal layout	Complex engineering plan

Buzz thinks he's a good technical salesman, but he's not. Engineers and buyers lose confidence when they see that Buzz has to call the factory for the answer to their questions or when the factory expert accompanies him on sales calls.

It may not be necessary for a salesperson to have an engineering background in order to sell technical products, but it is necessary for him or her to establish credibility early on. The rep must not only have the knowledge required to solve the customer's problem but must also *appear* to have enough knowledge to act as technical consultant and adviser.

If a buyer perceives that a salesperson is technically incompetent or may be incapable of bringing value to the project, the rep will never make it into the company's inner circle. This salesperson will be forever condemned to leaving messages on voice mail and reading copies of *Modern Material Handling* cover to cover in corporate lobbies.

Challenge #3: Salespeople must communicate on the buyer's terms. Technical buyers like people who can communicate on their terms. Fax machines, modems, computers, and CAD systems have accelerated the transmission of information. Buyers are demanding, and getting, instant information, in the form that they dictate. The requirements may include written reports (with excellent grammar), engineering drawings, well-thought-out business letters, and other formal means of communication.

Unfortunately, Buzz has limited communication skills. He can talk to anybody about anything, but when it comes to written communication, he falls short. He tries to avoid writing business letters, and his proposals are not well thought out.

In addition, Buzz is not comfortable with technology. He has never sat down at a computer or used a fax machine—even though he knows his customers like instant information. His excuse for his poor communications skills is that he wants to "spend time selling and getting orders, not doing secretarial work."

Challenge #4:   It takes multiple sales calls to win most business orders, and the sales cycle can take years.   A study by McGraw-Hill showed that it takes 4 to 4.5 calls to close an average industrial sale.[1] In the case of capital equipment sales or large projects, it may take multiple attempts to fund a project, and the sales cycle between quoting a job and delivering the product is often measured in years. Because of the rising cost of a sales call, the length of the sales cycle is becoming a more pressing problem in business marketing.

Buzz doesn't know the cost of each sales call he makes, nor does he understand that large accounts will take many calls to close. In his all-out efforts to find customers, he spends too much selling time getting small orders and making cold calls that don't justify his selling costs, and not enough time on potential large accounts.

Challenge #5:   Success in business-to-business selling is built on relationships.   In his book, *Rethinking Business to Business Marketing,* Paul Sherwood writes:

> A sales situation is much more likely to be successful—and, more important, be sustained—if there is a sense of relationship between the salesperson and the buyer. A somewhat elusive term to define, yet one we all understand, relationship suggests liking, a feeling of trust and mutual enhancement. It does not necessarily mean close social or personal interactions, but rather the feeling the customer might express as "I like him to come by. I like him, I trust him, I feel good when I'm with him, I learn something, and he always comes through for me." . . . The sales person must feel a respect and interest in the customer as a person—not as a money machine to be manipulated.[2]

Larry Maunder, vice president of sales for Cascade Corporation in Portland, Oregon, exemplifies the relationship philosophy more than anyone I have met in the marketing or sales game. He has been marketing lift truck attachments to dealers and OEMs for 32 years. He manages a field sales force of 23 district managers, who in turn manage more than 1,000 lift truck dealers in the United States and Canada. Maunder has worked his way up from salesman to the top job and has been involved in OEM alliances, private label agreements, major account sales, and dealer sales. Along the way, he has seen a wide variety of sales techniques and strategies. Maunder says that building relationships is the only effective long-term strategy for industrial selling, and the only way to generate repeat business.

Maunder spends a lot of his time in nonselling activities finding out all he can about his customers and what their problems are. He places a high value on building trust and displaying a willingness to back up customers.

Maunder believes that closing strategies and high-pressure tactics are simply gimmicks to get short-term orders, and that most of the time they don't work. He told me:

> Relationship selling is not about getting an order, it is about convincing customers that you will be there after the order, no matter what. Relationships are based on doing what is right, not doing whatever you can get away with. This is how we keep our dealers and their customers happy, and this is why we enjoy continuous growth.

Does this relationship-building strategy work? It has worked for Cascade Corporation. Cascade is the world's leading manufacturer of lift truck attachments. It continues to dominate in the US market, where competition is fierce. The company has experienced continuous growth and profitability for more than 30 years and owns approximately 70 percent of the world market for attachments. Maunder attributes much of the company's success to "the loyalty of independent dealers and the repeat business we enjoy year after year. Repeat business comes from excellent service and ongoing relationships."[3]

In contrast, Buzz Bigby doesn't strive to build relationships with his customers. "Customers," he likes to say, "are the guys between me and the order. I don't see sales as a personal commitment. It is a game of being able to read people and find their hot buttons. If you do it well, you can get rich."

Buzz views selling as a one-on-one contest between the salesperson and the buyer. He believes that guile, wit, charm, and tenacity are the hallmarks of a good salesman.

Buzz is totally focused on commissions, and customers can sense that his primary interest is in banking a check, not in helping them. Buzz works desperately hard to find customers who will give him orders, and places little emphasis on whether they will buy again. Not surprisingly, few of them do.

The five challenges of technical selling to large companies are difficult for someone like Buzz Bigby to face. Unless he addresses them—unless he develops his technical and communication skills, and learns how to build relationships rather than focus on commissions—Buzz (and other reps like him) is doomed to lose most of his rep contracts in the future. In the future, more and more business sales will be patterned on the scenario outlined above. Only salespeople who have the necessary skills to overcome the challenges of the large corporate selling environment will be able to succeed.

FOCUSING SELLING TIME

Now that you are aware of the complexities of selling to large corporations, let's focus on how you can get the most out of your limited selling time and budget. In most SMM companies there is a temptation to go for the quick sell, to engage in shotgun selling to any and every customer. The story of Industrial Power will illustrate the tremendous problems that arise when a company does not have a focused selling strategy.

Industrial Power, Inc., is a small manufacturer of motion control systems and sells a variety of hydraulic accessories. Industrial Power is a classic shotgun company. Cash flow is always a problem. The company has a large bank loan with heavy interest payments, and its salespeople are frustrated because they are not making the money they deserve. The company's sales plan is to increase sales somehow, but no matter how hard the sales force works, profitability is always elusive.

Industrial Power pulls in $10 million in sales each year from more than 3,000 accounts in a three-state area that is covered by seven factory reps. The company sells to large corporations such as paper mills, OEMS that use the products in their equipment, geographically scattered small customers, and even mom-and-pop companies that could just as easily buy their parts from a mail-order house.

Because there are so many small accounts, there are many collections problems and accounts in financial trouble. Few customers are satisfied with the product support they receive. Many of the salespeople who are responsible for large accounts that want engineered systems don't have the technical capability to manage them effectively.

The president of Industrial Products is convinced that face-to-face selling is the key to success. He doesn't like to see his reps spend time in the office or on the phone. He constantly tries to motivate them to increase the number of face-to-face cold calls they make and to creatively explore more companies.

Gordon Trotter is Industrial's Western Territory rep. Figure 9–2 shows Trotter's list of 350 accounts in three counties. About 40 customers account for 50 percent of his business. The other 310 customers account for 50 percent of his business, but 200 of these accounts are below $1,000 in annual sales volume. Despite their differences, all customers get the same amount of coverage. Trotter's repeat business rate is not good, partly because these accounts make demands for products and services that he can't supply.

Gordon Trotter's efforts to develop a profitable sales territory are plaqued by problems that are typical of a shotgun selling strategy. Trotter doesn't know who the MVCs in his territory are. Since the company has no marketing plan, he doesn't know which market niches the company wants him to focus time on. He doesn't have the training to handle the large accounts in his territory effectively. Nor has he developed cost-effective ways to reach small or marginal accounts.

Trotter spends little time qualifying accounts on the phone or by letter. He spends most of his time on the road, making face-to-face calls to please the boss. He is loyal to all his customers, regardless of sales volume or location, and he once drove 4 hours to take a $100 seal kit to a customer on the coast. No one in the company has ever tried to calculate the cost of a sales call.

Gordon Trotter is frustrated with the large paper mills in his territory, and has not made much headway in selling to them. These customers always want engineering help and systems, and never seem to be willing to buy any of the products shown in his three-ring binder. There are many people involved in the buying process, and there's lots of paperwork and meetings. Trotter knows he can't waste time with these companies when there are no orders forthcoming; he must get out and find more companies who can buy.

Trotter has concluded that since Industrial Power doesn't have a plan, he must devise his own strategy to try to improve his income. Since he is paid a commission based on gross selling price, company profitability is not a primary concern for him; getting the order is.

FIGURE 9–2
Industrial Power Inc., Gordon Trotter's Account List: 350 Accounts

	Customer Address	Year-to-Date Sales
Top 20% MVCs: 12 customers	ADEK	$155,000
	OECO	133,100
	Puget	22,300
	Hyster	29,780
	PCC	26,780
	FLIR	30,000
	Boise	48,000
	TEK	39,000
	Warn	46,000
	Allied	36,000
	Aptec	24,000
	Blount	15,000
138 other customers	ABC	1,200
	Delta	1,890
	Brown	5,400
	Intech	4,890
	Action	3,456
	Steel	2,456
	Hanson	4,980
	Mamoth	1,200
	.	.
	.	.
	.	.
200 small customers	Gemini	560
	Thurston	900
	ABC Inc.	560
	Gemstone	900
	Eastside	200
	MFB Inc.	340
	Maybrook	235
	Welloms	300
	Alltech	245

The Solution to Industrial Power's Problems

The way to solve the problems of Industrial Power and other, similar shotgun companies is to go through a step-by-step process to build a comprehensive, cost-based, profit-oriented sales strategy. The process is described below.

Step 1.   Determine the cost of a face-to-face sales call.   Definitions of the cost of a sales call differ by industry and company, the size of a territory, and the way it is covered. Some companies simply calculate salary costs and miscellaneous expenses; others add an overhead factor as part of the cost.

Sales & Marketing Magazine (S&MM) offers the most comprehensive estimates of the cost of an industrial sale, in their annual publication, *A User's Guide to the Sales Manager's Budget Planner.*[4] *S&MM* gathers data from a wide array of industrial goods industries. It bases its calculations on two different types of sales territories: (1) a large metropolitan area where customers are tightly concentrated and (2) a large territory where customers are widely dispersed and the salesperson must spend considerable time traveling.

The annual *S&MM* survey for 1992 reveals that, in a heavily concentrated territory, an industrial sales rep can make between 561 and 935 calls per year. In a larger territory, reps average from 374 to 748 calls per year.

The survey also shows that the cost of an industrial sales rep (including compensation and expenses) in 1992 ranged from $25,000 to $160,000 for the two types of territories. From this data, *S&MM* calculated that the average cost of an industrial sales call in 1992 was $227.27.

Figure 9–3 shows the calculated costs of one of Industrial Power's sales reps. Each rep has a car and is paid a base salary plus commission. Each rep is responsible for 300 to 400 accounts scattered over a territory that requires driving as far away as 100 miles.

The average rep costs the company about $56,000 per year in compensation and expenses, and can make a maximum of 750 face-to-face calls in the territory per year, including cold calls. This averages out to about $75 per sales call.

You must be careful about using national figures because local sales costs vary a great deal. To put this national estimate into perspective, Figure 9–4 shows the cost of a sales call for three different kinds of products and sales territories (T1, T2, and T3). As the figure shows, costs can vary substantially.

Step 2.   Determine the sales volume required to cover sales costs.   Calculating the cost of a sales call is the first step in developing a territory sales plan. The next step is to determine the minimum sales required for each account in the territory to be profitable. Not all accounts

FIGURE 9–3
Industrial Power Inc., Sales Call Cost Analysis

Annual Sales Compensation	
Salary (base)	$24,000
Commission	12,000
Taxes and insurance @ 15%	5,000
Benefits @ 10%	3,000
Total compensation	$44,000
Sales Expenses	
Travel	$ 1,000
Auto	2,400
Mileage	1,600
Meals and entertainment	5,000
Hotels and miscellaneous	2,000
Total expenses	$12,000
Total direct sales costs	$56,000
Maximum face-to-face calls per year	750

> Average cost per call $75

FIGURE 9–4
Sales Cost Comparisons

T1 Industrial distributor salesman with local one-county territory and a car, selling valves.
Calls per year	750
Sales call cost	$75/call

T2 Independent rep covering Michigan and Ohio, using a car and occasional airplane travel, selling capital equipment.
Calls per year	450
Sales call cost	$150/call

T3 Factory district rep covering several states and 300 dealers, with a car and airplane travel, selling crusher wear parts (castings).
Calls per year	500
Sales call cost	$200/call

FIGURE 9–5
Industrial Power Inc., Sales Cost Justification

Minimum sales calls per order	3
Sales expense to sales revenue ratio	10%
Minimum sales per account	
Average cost per order	
(3 calls × $75 cost per call)	$ 225
Cost per order: sales expense	
($225 ÷ 10%)	2,250
Breakeven territory sales	
Total direct costs per year	$ 56,000
Direct costs ÷ sales expense	
$56,000 ÷ 10%	560,000

justify face-to-face selling. By comparing selling costs to revenues generated, it's possible to determine which accounts are profitable and which are not.

One way to project the minimum expected revenues per account is shown in Figure 9–5. As this figure shows, at Industrial Power, sales expenses average about 10 percent of sales, and it takes three calls, on average, to close an order.

Multiplying the cost per call by the minimum number of calls required to make a sale and then dividing this figure by 10 percent shows that the Industrial Power rep needs to generate $2,225 per account in order to break even and justify the cost of face-to-face sales calls.

To calculate the breakeven figure for the company as a whole, simply take the total sales cost figure for one rep ($56,000) and divide it by 10 percent, as in Figure 9–5. The figure shows that each territory must generate $560,000 in revenues in order for Industrial Power to cover the cost of the rep assigned to the territory.

This is a crucial figure. If a territory can produce only $300,000 in sales per year, or if the total sales volume varies significantly from year to year, the company might be better off exploring other, less costly sales channel possibilities.

Step 3.   Identify the MVCs and search for similar customers.
In Industrial Power's rush to find more customers and more sales, there is
little time left either to identify the most valuable customers or to develop
strategies for prospecting for more accounts like them.

If Industrial Power wants to become profitable, it will have to identify
its MVCs (as outlined in Chapter 2), learn about their needs, develop a
profile of their characteristics, and search for more customers like them.
This targeted approach will dramatically improve the company's chances
of selling success.

Step 4.   Set call frequency and priorities.   Let's return for a
moment to the Industrial Power example. Gordon Trotter has been making roughly 750 sales calls a year, many of them to relatively small accounts. His company has identified its large accounts, has selected
accounts in the paper industry and certain OEMs as the MVCs, and has
instructed Trotter to make a concerted effort to improve sales and generate repeat business with these accounts. Management accepts the fact that
sales calls on these large accounts require more time, and that the number
of face-to-face calls Trotter will make under this new approach will inevitably fall, to around 500 calls a year.

Figure 9–6 shows the method Gordon Trotter used to set his account
priorities and sales call frequency, by separating MVCs from less profitable accounts. He began by listing all the accounts in the territory according to sales volume (year-to-date, or YTD), and profitability. Then he
indicated the sales potential of the account, based on past performance
and growth trends, and noted whether the account is a MVC and/or a repeat customer, or is a target niche account. Finally, he noted the total
number of calls required to achieve the annual sales goal for each customer, in the last column on the right.

As Figure 9–6 shows, Trotter estimated it will take 252 calls just to cover
his MVCs, and another 250 calls to effectively handle 138 other accounts.

Gordon Trotter will be able to make only about 500 face-to-face calls a
year. What should he and his company do with the accounts that don't
warrant face-to-face calls, either because the revenue they generate is low,
or because they are geographically scattered or distant? What about the
very large accounts and OEMS that require more services than Trotter can
offer? How should the company handle the customers that buy only small
parts and accessories? For these accounts, Industrial Power will have to
find alternative sales channels.

FIGURE 9–6
Territory Analysis (*Setting Sales Priorities*)

Customer Address	YTD Sales	YTD Profit	Sales Potential	Niche Priority	Target or MVC Account	Repeat Customer	Call Frequency per year
High-Volume Accounts (12)							
Adek	$155,000	40%	$150,000	OEM		X	24
OECO	133,100	34	200,000	OEM	X	X	24
Puget	122,300	30	100,000	OEM		X	24
Hyster	119,780	34	120,000	OEM		X	24
PCC	116,780	29	10,000				12
FLIR	110,000	12	30,000				12
Boise	108,000	24	100,000	Paper	X	X	24
TEK	89,000	34	150,000		X		24
Warn	76,000	40	80,000	OEM	X		24
Allied	66,000	41	50,000	OEM	X		24
Crown	54,000	32	100,000	Paper	X	X	24
Blount	45,000	26	5,000				12
Total calls							252
Other Important Accounts (138)							
International	1,200		6,000	Paper	X	X	12
Delta	1,890		2,000				6
James	5,400		10,000	Paper	X	X	24
Intech	4,890		9,000		X		12
Action	3,456		1,000	OEM			6
Steel	2,456		2,000				3
Hanson	4,980		5,000	OEM			12
:							:
Total calls							250
Total calls per year							502
All Other Accounts							
Gemstone	900		900				2
Eastside	200		200				0
MFB Inc.	340		1,000				2
Proturn	560		1,000				2
ICE	123		500	OEM			1
Ramey	650		650	OEM			1
:							:

FIGURE 9–7

Channels-of-Distribution Grid (*Industrial Power's Hybrid Approach*)

Channel	Sales Tasks				Customer Niche
	Qualify propect	Presale information	Closing sale	Postsale service	
National accounts		▨	▨	▨	Large corporate accounts
Direct sales		▨	▨	▨	Top MVCs
Independent representatives	▨	▨	▨		Geographically scattered accounts
Telemarketing	▨	▨	▨		Low volume accounts
Mail order catalog	▨	▨	▨		Parts customers

Step 5. Identify alternative sales channel possibilities. Alternative channel options were reviewed in Chapter 7, and the idea of hybrid channel solutions was introduced. This is a cost-effective solution that Industrial Power might consider in order to cover the accounts that are not profitably managed by the direct sales force. Specifically, the company could divide its accounts into four categories, and develop a different channel solution for each category, as described below. (See Figure 9–7.)

National accounts. Industrial Power has two large OEMs and several large corporations that want special products and services, ranging from applications engineering to annual purchasing contracts. One way to service these large accounts would be through a national account team consisting of sales, service, and technical personnel who would interact with purchasing, manufacturing, engineering, and other decision makers in the large organizations.

Direct sales. With the large corporate accounts taken care of, the direct salespeople could focus their face-to-face selling time on MVCs and prospective MVCs. If there was not enough selling time available to cover all the high-potential accounts, perhaps another direct salesperson could be added or Trotter could modify his call frequency schedule, so that he wouldn't visit each high-priority customer as often as in the past.

Independent reps.   Industrial Power is losing money on some of the products it sells to geographically scattered accounts. These accounts might best be handled by independent reps, or by a factory salesperson who is allowed to sell other lines as well. The challenge will be managing the independent reps and avoiding conflict with the direct salespeople.

Telemarketing.   The telemarketing approach used by Chuck Martin at Hampton Power Products (see Chapter 7) would also work well for Industrial Power. Telemarketing could be used to manage the smaller accounts and to support the field sales people. The telemarketing department could focus on accounts under $2,000 and could make market development calls in designated niches. The department could also help the field salespeople by identifying the key decision makers, sending out literature and catalogs, identifying and qualifying sales leads, and setting up field sales visits.

Mail-order or catalog sales.   Some of the smaller accounts that order individual parts and accessories could be managed through a catalog designed specifically for their applications and needs. A mail-order approach to these customers could be used to send presale information and to close orders, if the accounts were carefully targeted and prices were comparable to those in competitive catalogs.

Step 6.   Qualify all prospects by phone before making face-to-face calls.   Many salespeople prefer the buyer/seller chemistry of the face-to-face sales pitch over the impersonal sound of an unknown voice at the other end of a phone line. For many reps, the physical action of driving around and making calls creates a false impression that they are getting things done, regardless of their sales results. This is particularly true of salespeople in a shotgun selling program in which there are rewards for cold calls and auto mileage gets confused with sales productivity.

The high cost of the average industrial sales call makes it vital to qualify customers on the phone. Qualifying prospects by telephone saves money and effectively focuses face-to-face selling time. As discussed in

Chapter 7, an inside telemarketing or sales department can be set up to qualify all leads, probe markets, open new accounts, and schedule visits for the field salespeople. If you don't have the luxury of a telemarketing department and your salespeople have to qualify prospects by phone, here are some suggestions for them.

1. Define "qualified." Get the salespeople together and ask them what kind of prospects should warrant a personal call. In general, a qualified lead or prospect is someone who has a need for the product, has a budget for the product or is planning to request funding, and either has the authority to buy or is a member of the DMU that will make the purchase.

2. Conduct a qualification interview. Develop a list of questions for salespeople to ask in order to qualify each prospect. (Make sure each salesperson learns the basic interviewing tactics discussed in Chapter 3.) Probe the prospect about applications, short- and long-term needs, purchasing authority, and the time line for the purchase.

The easiest way to qualify a prospect is to follow up after sending literature. Following is a typical conversation between George Pillsbury, a factory sales engineer at Portable Machine Inc., and Paul Davis, a prospect at Crown Paper Mill. Davis was sent a catalog the week before, and Pillsbury is calling to find out whether there is any sales potential at Crown.

The greeting

George:

Good morning. Is Paul Davis in? [*George is connected to Paul's extension.*] Good morning, Paul, this is George Pillsbury with Portable Machines in Alameda, California. Last week I sent you a catalog of our portable machine tools for on-site maintenance. Did you receive the information?

Paul:

Yes, I remember seeing it come in last week.

Establish a need

George:

The purpose of my call today is to speak with you about portable machine tools. Do you ever have a need to do machining on the production machines out on the floor?

Paul:

Well, we always try to get the parts into our machine shop or send them out locally. But some of the shafts are very big and expensive and dangerous to move. Why? Do you have something that works in the plant?

Explore applications

George:

We have a portable lathe that can turn a 24-inch shaft, and in fact have sold these lathes to many paper mills like yours. What kind of machines are you talking about and what diameter shafts? [*The conversation continues as the men discuss various applications.*]

Determine whether the buyer is qualified

George:

Paul, can I ask what your job title is, and what you do at Crown Paper?

Paul:

I'm an engineer and I work in the plant engineering department. I buy some new equipment, but mostly I'm responsible for maintaining and upgrading the production line.

George:

Does that mean you put together capital requests and buy equipment?

Paul:

I don't actually issue the purchase order, but I tell the purchasing department what I want to buy, and I write the specifications and send in the request for funds.

Determine the budget

George:

Would you be interested in exploring this portable lathe idea if it could save you money?

Paul:

Well, I don't have a project right now, but if I could see a payback of less than a year and if it would save a lot of the downtime that it now takes to machine a big shaft off site, I might be interested.

George:

If the payback is there, how do you go about getting these kinds of projects funded?

Paul:

If the project is under $50,000, we could probably buy it in our maintenance budget, but the project would have to have a very good payback because there are a lot of requests right now.

The close

George:

I'd like to fax you some more information about the model PL1174 portable lathe, and an information form. If you'll fill out the form with the basic specs on the machine and shaft, we'll put together a proposal and find out if it could save you some time and money. [*The conversation continues about fax numbers and the information needed.*]

George:

All right then, I'll fax the information today. If you need any help or have questions when you get the form, please give me a call at our 800 number.

3. Send information immediately. Send out the literature or response package immediately. The response package can be varied to fit the needs of the prospect, but it should always include a cover letter that contains all appropriate phone and fax numbers, the appropriate catalogs, and a return card to make it easy for the prospect to get back in touch with you.

4. Take action. If the prospect is a qualified buyer, take action now. Either set up an appointment to visit or turn the lead over to a salesperson who can call on the prospect before your competitors do.

5. Follow up. Record all interview information in a database or follow-up system that includes a follow-up date. Make sure that the salesperson closes the loop and records the results of the call. At this point, the company has invested a lot of money in the new prospect, and you need to know whether the program is working. You also need to find out whether your advertising or other lead generation programs are effective or should be modified.

Some professionals believe that a letter is more effective than a follow-up phone call in paving the way for a face-to-face call on a qualified prospect. A well-written letter has several advantages over a telephone call:

- The impact of a letter lasts longer, because the prospect has the time to read and think about the ideas it presents.
- A letter gives the salesperson time to compose the selling points and customize them for that specific prospect. The fact that you've taken the time to craft a letter that is targeted to the prospect's specific needs sends a message of professionalism that would not be communicated so effectively in a phone call.
- If the customer is a large corporation, a letter is the perfect vehicle for proposing an agenda for a meeting with all members of the DMU.
- A letter can summarize points that may require a lot of time on the phone. This is important, since many buyers are extremely busy and don't want to spend much time on the phone with you.
- A letter saves time during the actual sales call, because it covers many of the normal preliminaries ahead of time.

Step 7.   Allocate time and money for market and product development calls.   Now you have focused your face-to-face selling time on your most profitable customers and assigned marginal accounts to less expensive channels. The tasks that remain are to probe new markets, to prospect for new customers, and to help the factory sell new products. If you have a telemarketing department to qualify leads, this group might also take over market development calls. This is more cost-effective than the traditional approach of having direct salespeople do the development work.

What if you don't have a telemarketing department, and your company uses independent sales reps who don't get paid unless they sell something? Obviously, independent reps will be reluctant to make "missionary" calls in new markets or for new products, because these calls would take away from the time they spend making calls that will lead to commissions.

Market and product development calls provide necessary information for the factory to develop new products and new markets. The probability that these "missionary" calls will produce quick sales is remote, yet the calls will come directly out of the independent rep's precious face-to-face selling time. Since these calls are more vital to the factory than to the rep, several independent rep and distributor organizations suggest that reps should receive additional compensation for them.

An increasing number of manufacturers are doing just this. The Manufacturer's Agents National Association conducted surveys of its members
in 1984 and 1991 on the issue of compensation for new product calls. The
survey asked, "Do principals pay higher commission for new product introduction?" In 1984, 30 percent of the principals in the survey said they
offered a higher commission for introducing new products; by 1991, that
figure had jumped to 40 percent. The survey also found that the additional
compensation for new product development activities could be in the
form of advances on commissions, or other special incentives.[5]

*   *   *   *   *

By now you understand the hazards of shotgun marketing. You have
learned how to profile your customers, how to conduct interviews, and
how to gather competitive and market intelligence. I have covered the basics of niche marketing, and have described the benefits and the process
of customer-driven product development. You have learned about a variety of distribution channel alternatives, as well as strategies for advertising effectively on a shoestring budget. In this chapter, I have explored the
ways in which successful SMMs focus their face-to-face selling time on
their most profitable customers. Now it's time to incorporate all this information into a practical marketing plan that can guide your day-to-day operations.

KEY POINT

Many SMMs are struggling with increasing selling costs and constantly
changing customer demands for products and services. For a company to
be profitable in this environment, it must carefully focus face-to-face selling time on the accounts that have the greatest potential for future sales.

SUGGESTED ACTION

Have your salespeople calculate how many face-to-face sales calls they
make a year, and how many calls are needed to close the average order.
Use this information to calculate the average cost of a sales call. Then,
using the formula presented in Figure 9–5, determine how much sales
volume is needed to break even in the territory, and how much volume it

takes for any given account to justify a face-to-face call. This will give enough data to help your salespeople develop a sales strategy that focuses face-to-face selling time on high-potential customers and delegates less profitable accounts to less costly sales channels.

NOTES

1. *LAP Reports 8013 and 8051* (New York: McGraw-Hill).
2. *Rethinking Business to Business Marketing* by Paul Sherlock. Copyright © 1991 by Paul Sherlock. Reprinted with the permission of The Free Press, a Division of Macmillan, Inc.
3. Interview with Larry Maunder, July 1993.
4. "A User's Guide to the Sales Manager's Budget Planner," *Sales and Marketing Management,* June 28, 1993, pp. 6–10.
5. "Compensating Agents for Pioneering New Products," *Agency Sales Magazine,* January 1991, pp. 5–9.

Chapter Ten

The Marketing Plan
A Small Investment with a Big Payoff

"I know we need a marketing plan, but we just don't have the time or money to develop one." That's the response of most owners and managers of SMMs when asked whether or not they have a marketing plan. It's true that many small and midsize manufacturing companies don't have much time to plan. It's also a fact that most SMMs operate on an extremely tight budget. However, they do seem to find time and money to develop new products, buy new machine tools, make cold calls, generate advertising inquiries, attend trade shows, and drive or fly hundreds or thousands of miles—all in the name of increasing sales. It's not unreasonable to suggest they spend **one day a year** developing a marketing plan that would make the most of their revenue-generating activities.

No SMM can afford to call on the wrong customers, advertise to the wrong markets, or design the wrong products. The best way to make the most of your limited resources is to take time to develop a well-thought-out marketing plan.

A marketing plan doesn't have to be complicated to be effective. It doesn't have to be a lengthy treatise on everything you know about customers and markets. In fact, it can be as brief as a single page. All it has to do is communicate the basics: what marketing activities should be pursued, how much they will cost, and who will be responsible for implementing them.

It's not even absolutely necessary to have a written plan (although I recommend it). Many SMMs have done very well without written marketing plans, but few have succeeded without some form of a plan, however simple—even if it is only stored in the mind of the owner and communicated verbally to employees.

If you dread the thought of writing a marketing plan, dictate your plan into a tape recorder, scribble the main points on an envelope, call a meeting to describe the plan to employees, make a video, or find some other way to communicate it. It doesn't matter what form your plan takes; the important thing is that you have a plan.

In the following pages, I'll provide two examples of marketing plans. The basis of the first plan is a simple one-page budget; the second example is a complex plan of the type that is found in detailed business plans designed to attract investors. You might follow one of these options, or develop something in between. What's important is that you draft a plan that meets your needs—a plan that will enable you to get the most benefit out of your limited marketing budget.

EXAMPLE 1:   PROMILL MACHINE INC.: A SIMPLE BUSINESS MARKETING PLAN

Promill Machine Inc. is a small, family-owned company that offers a wide variety of high-quality machining, assembly, and fabrication services to other SMMs. The 10-year-old company employs 50 people.

Promill started as a one-man shop and has grown to become a $2 million company. Unfortunately, much of this growth resulted from a shotgun marketing strategy that attracted 105 customers with widely differing needs. Now Promill is having trouble satisfying all these different customers. Customer demands are already straining the production system. To make matters worse, some of the larger customers are demanding that Promill acquire ISO 9000 quality certification, which would require a total overhaul of all the company's production systems and a major investment in time.

Because of these problems, Promill decided it was time to do some serious rethinking of its marketing strategy. A careful review of the company's records showed that five customers, in two market niches—OEMs and paper mills—accounted for 65 percent of sales and profits. These are Promill's MVCs. Not only are they the highest revenue producers, but these MVCs have the most potential to buy complete automation machines (instead of just parts) and to give Promill annual contracts.

The owners decided to redesign their production and quality systems based on the needs of these MVCs rather than on the needs of all 105 customers—and they set out to find more valuable customers like the MVCs.

They consulted a manufacturing directory that turned up 50 target companies in the OEM and paper mill niches. Now that they knew how many companies were in their target market niches, the owners thought about what they would need to do in order to win the business of these potentially valuable companies.

To reach these prospects, the owners knew they would need to hire an outside salesperson. They figured they would have to contract with a telemarketing firm, develop a company brochure and specification sheets, and attend a trade show. Their plans also called for mailing information to prospect companies and taking advantage of free publicity in trade journals.

With this information in hand, the owners put together a marketing plan in the form of a simple, one-page profit and loss (P&L) statement and a marketing budget for the coming year (Figure 10–1). Developing this simple P&L and budget was a major step for Promill Machines, which had never before estimated its revenues or forecast its marketing expenses.

Once the budget was developed, the owners assigned the responsibility for the various marketing activities required to meet the forecast to individual employees. After only six months, this simple marketing plan began returning dividends to the company, in the form of increased inquiries and requests for quotes, and the possibility of landing orders from several large OEM accounts.

EXAMPLE 2:   A DETAILED BUSINESS MARKETING PLAN

If you own or manage a midsize manufacturing company and have a marketing staff, a reasonable budget, and planning experience, you might consider developing a more detailed marketing plan. Typically, companies develop fairly sophisticated marketing plans when they are searching for more investors or additional capital, or when they are in the high-risk situation of developing new products for new markets.

This type of plan is at the opposite end of the spectrum from Promill's one-page approach. It includes a detailed market analysis section that analyzes the customers, competitors, and market niches and describes the market opportunities. This information is used to develop a marketing strategies section that carefully details product, price, promotion, and sales strategies for taking advantage of the market opportunities. Since there is usually a lot of money at stake, the plan must also provide detailed financial information, including a pro forma sales forecast and an income statement.

FIGURE 10–1
Simple P&L and Marketing Budget (*Promill Machine Inc.*)

	$000 Year
Sales projection	2,000
Cost of goods sold	1,200
Gross margin	800
Expenses, nonmarketing	500
Marketing expenses	
Sales (one direct salesperson)	60
Commissions	10
Service and warranty	20
Telemarketing service	10
Literature	
Brochure	3
Spec sheets	3
Product bulletins	2
Application reports	1
Advertising	
Trade journal ads	0
Direct mail	
Customer mailing	5
Trade show	
Small booth at Seattle, Washington, show	5
Publicity	
Product releases (six)	1
Trade journal story (writing)	1
Total marketing budget	121
Total expense	621
Profit (EBIT)	179

The outline given later in this chapter can be used to develop a detailed marketing plan. The outline is in the form of questions that must be answered and instructions that must be followed for each element in the market analysis and marketing strategies sections. The outline includes numerous references to other parts of this book that will be helpful in answering the questions and developing the plan. I've also provided a sample pro forma income statement and a sales forecast (Figure 10–2) you can use as a guide in developing your own pro forma statement and forecast.

FIGURE 10–2
Pro Forma Income Statement (*in Thousands of $*)

	January	February	March	April	May	June
Sales	$3,400.21	$3,947.71	$3,243.19	$4,056.24	$3,962.26	$3,230.20
Cost of goods sold						
Product costs	2,386.40	2,890.90	2,574.80	2,705.60	2,695.10	2,267.08
Inventory revaluation	50.00	50.00	50.00	50.00	50.00	50.00
Over/under absorbed	(73.20)	158.30	84.50	55.10	(120.00)	(69.54)
Transportation	(4.20)	(14.40)	(38.30)	46.40	0.30	(3.99)
Equipment manuals	10.00	10.20	7.80	13.60	15.50	9.50
Warranty	38.50	29.70	126.30	120.60	77.60	36.58
	2,407.50	3,124.70	2,805.10	2,991.30	2,718.50	2,289.63
Gross profit	992.71	823.01	438.09	1,064.94	1,243.76	940.57
Marketing expenses						
Sales salaries	301.70	337.60	387.90	351.10	231.90	286.62
Service salaries	94.20	133.60	158.70	136.40	174.60	89.49
Rep commissions	170.01	197.39	162.16	202.81	198.11	161.51
Advertising	12.50	10.56	8.90	7.50	11.10	11.88
Trade show						
literature	9.18	10.66	8.76	10.95	10.70	8.72
	587.59	689.81	726.42	708.76	626.41	558.22
Administration	104.80	70.40	73.00	150.00	223.20	99.56
Nonoperating	54.40	12.70	89.30	76.70	(38.50)	51.68
Product liability	46.00	48.80	99.30	99.90	66.20	43.70
R&D	14.00	16.20	7.80	54.20	34.60	13.30
	219.20	148.10	269.40	380.80	285.50	208.24
Total expenses	806.79	837.91	995.82	1,089.56	911.91	766.46
Pretax profit (loss)	$185.92	($14.90)	($557.73)	($24.62)	$331.85	$174.11

For more detailed information about how to develop an income statement and a marketing budget, see Philip G. Duffy's *Business to Business
Marketing.*[1] For the SMM that has never grappled with pro forma income
statements and budgets, I recommend *The Entrepreneur's Master Planning Guide* by John A. Welsh and Jerry F. White, which outlines an easy,
step-by-step approach to the process.[2]

One caution before you begin: The danger in developing formal
marketing plans is that they can take on a life of their own; the plan becomes an end in itself, rather than a tool for use in achieving your marketing goals. As you develop your detailed marketing plan, make sure

FIGURE 10–2 (*concluded*)
Pro Forma Income Statement (*in Thousands of $*)

	July	August	September	October	November	December	Fiscal Year Total
	\$4,539.86	\$2,983.74	\$4,867.49	\$4,081.12	\$3,553.22	\$4,312.87	\$46,178.11
	3,324.54	2,368.82	2,570.32	2,775.95	1,995.03	3,158.31	
	50.00	50.00	50.00	50.00	50.00	50.00	
	182.05	77.74	52.35	(123.60)	(61.20)	172.94	
	(16.56)	(35.24)	44.08	0.31	(3.51)	(15.73)	
	11.73	7.18	12.92	15.97	8.36	11.14	
	34.16	116.20	114.57	79.93	32.19	32.45	
	3,585.92	2,584.70	2,844.24	2,798.56	2,020.87	3.409.11	33,580.13
	953.94	399.04	2,023.25	1,282.56	1,532.35	903.76	12,597.98
	303.84	310.32	333.55	238.86	252.22	288.65	
	120.24	126.96	129.58	179.84	78.75	114.23	
	226.99	149.19	243.37	204.06	177.66	215.64	
	9.50	7.12	7.13	11.43	10.45	9.03	
					100.00		
	12.26	8.06	13.14	11.02	9.59	11.64	
	672.83	601.65	726.77	645.21	628.67	639.19	7,811.53
	63.36	58.40	142.50	229.90	87.61	60.19	
	11.43	71.44	72.87	(39.66)	45.48	10.86	
	43.92	79.44	94.91	68.19	38.46	41.72	
	14.58	6.24	51.49	35.64	11.70	13.85	
	133.29	215.52	361.77	294.07	183.25	126.62	2,825.76
	806.12	817.17	1,088.54	939.28	811.92	765.81	10,637.29
	\$147.82	(\$418.13)	\$934.71	\$343.28	\$720.43	\$137.95	\$1,960.69

you build common sense into the process and limit the number of pages. No one—including investors—will read a 100-page marketing plan.

To simplify the process (if you are not planning to submit the plan to potential investors), instead of preparing a written plan, consider summarizing each section of the plan on a one-page graphic that you can project onto a screen. Each of these pages or transparencies should show your abbreviated responses to the questions or instructions below; you can summarize the rest of your plan verbally.

DETAILED 12-MONTH MARKETING PLAN

Market Analysis

A. Customers
   1. Who are your MVCs? What are their profiles? (See Figure 2–1, "Basic Customer Database," and Figure 2–2, "Comprehensive Business Marketing Database.")
   2. Which customers and prospects are buying your competitors' products? Why? (See "Lost Order Analysis" in Chapter 2).
   3. Provide an example of how your products and services are meeting your customers' needs. (See Figure 2–4, "The Acid Test.")
   4. Show results of a recent customer survey that provides evidence that you are satisfying customers. (See sample surveys, Figures 2–4, 2–5, and 2–6).

B. Competition
   1. Who are your direct competitors?
   2. Compare your competitors' products to your own, showing the strengths and weaknesses of each. (See Figure 4–1, "The Competitive Matrix.")
   3. Who are your indirect competitors? What do you know about them? (See the discussion of substitute products in Chapter 6.)
   4. Show how customers compare your company to competitors. (See Figure 4–2, "Ask a Customer.")
   5. Describe your strategy for taking business from the competitors.

C. Market
   1. Describe your market niches in terms of SIC Codes, products purchased, customer size, industry, or other relevant factors.
   2. Estimate the number of customers and prospects in each targeted market niche. Rank the niches in order of importance, and explain your ranking.
   3. Describe the major trends in each market niche.
   4. Describe the competitors in each niche. List the top three competitors, in terms of estimated annual revenues. Explain how you calculated estimated revenues.
   5. If possible, estimate the future sales potential in each niche. Show the reasoning behind your estimates.

Marketing Strategies

A. Marketing costs and opportunities
   1. Using "The Shotgun Checklist" (Figure 1–2), identify current marketing strategy problems and opportunities for cost savings or improved efficiency.

B. Product plan
   1. Describe your product lines in terms of sales growth and user benefits. (See Figure 6–6, "User Benefit Checklist.")
   2. Describe new products under development, and indicate whether they are line extensions, replacements or substitutes, or leading-edge products. (See "The Three Basic Product Types" in Chapter 6.) Describe the customer needs the products satisfy. (See Figure 6–5, "Screening Matrix.")
   3. Describe the risks involved in new product development, and show how the products under development match company strengths. (See "Step 4. Make a Reality Check: How Much Can You Afford to Gamble?" in Chapter 6.)
   4. Describe the services that will be included in the product package, and explain why they are needed. (See "Step 9. Develop the Product/Service Package" in Chapter 6.)
   5. Identify mature products with declining sales, and describe your plan to phase these products out or replace them with new products.

C. Distribution plan
   1. Describe the current channels of distribution and the customers they reach.
   2. Outline the selling costs, commissions, discounts, and gross margins associated with each distribution channel. (See examples of sales call costs in Figure 9–4, breakeven formulas in Figure 9–5), and cost-of-sale estimates in Figures 7–4 and 9–3.)
   3. Explain the strengths and weaknesses of each channel's performance, and your plan for improving your channel strategy. (See Figure 7–5, "Distributor Performance Scale"; Figure 7–6, "Rep Performance Scale"; and Figure 7–8, "The Do's and Don'ts of Working with Independents.")
   4. Explain the strengths and weaknesses of your factory support program and show how you plan to improve it. (See Figure 7–7, "Factory Performance Scale.")

     5. Explain how you will change your distribution strategy in the future to accommodate different types of customers and increases or decreases in channel costs. (See Figure 9–7.)

D. Sales plan

     1. Explain how your sales and distribution strategies will accommodate large-customer accounts, accounts with many decision makers, buyers who require considerable technical information, sophisticated buyers, and projects requiring many sales calls and a long sales cycle. (See "The Five Realities of Selling to Large Corporations," in Chapter 9.)

     2. Explain how you will establish relationships with MVCs in order to improve repeat business.

     3. Explain how sales territories are established, and the cost justifications for them. (See Figure 9–5, "Industrial Power Inc.: Sales Cost Justification.")

     4. Describe your sales strategy in terms of sales priorities and call frequency. (See Figure 9–6, "Territory Analysis: Setting Sales Priorities.")

     5. Describe the sales strategies necessary for developing new markets (see Chapter 5) or introducing new products (see Chapter 6).

     6. Show an example of sales quotation activity, including your success rate (or "hit rate"), and explain what steps you will take to improve the hit rate.

E. Pricing

     1. Describe the basis for your current and future pricing.

     2. Describe the pricing strategy you use to gain an advantage over competitors in specific market niches.

F. Advertising and promotion plan

     1. Describe your overall strategy for generating leads, and provide an estimate of the number of leads necessary to achieve your sales forecast.

     2. Describe the measurement system that will be used to evaluate each advertising or direct mail piece in terms of cost justification and direct connection to the sales effort. (See Chapter 8.)

     3. Describe your strategy for each of the following, and show how each focuses on targeted market niches:

       a. Trade journal advertising.

   b. Publicity and product releases.
   c. Direct mail advertising.
   d. Literature and spec sheets.
   e. Trade shows.
 G. Service and warranty plan
  1. Describe your service department, and explain how the warranty and service programs will ensure product quality and fit into your overall strategy for satisfying customers. (See the Chapter 11 discussion of service quality and customer perceptions, and work through Figure 11–1, "Customer Services Checklist.") Describe how your warranty and service programs will ensure product quality and customer satisfaction.
  2. Describe a program that will continuously monitor all warranty and customer satisfaction problems. (See "Eight Simple Ways to Monitor Customer Satisfaction" in Chapter 11.)

*   *   *   *   *

You have now labored through the whole marketing process and capped it off with a marketing plan. Congratulations! The only thing left for me to do is to show you, in Chapter 11, how to apply all the ideas presented in this book in order to achieve the most important goal of all: total customer satisfaction.

KEY POINT

Since limited resources are a fact of life for most SMMs, these companies must invest their marketing dollars where they will generate the highest return. The best way to accomplish this is to first invest some time in developing a marketing plan.

SUGGESTED ACTION

Assign someone the task of creating a 12-month pro forma income statement—either a simple P&L statement and a budget (see Figure 10–1) or a complex income statement (see Figure 10–2). Then, gather all managers and key employees together for a day away from the office, and develop a basic marketing plan.

NOTES

1. Philip G Duffy, *B to B Marketing: Creating and Implementing a Successful Business to Business Marketing Program* (Chicago: Probus Publishing, 1992).

2. John A Welsh and Jerry F White, *The Entrepreneur's Master Planning Guide* (Englewood Cliffs, NJ: Prentice Hall, 1983).

Chapter Eleven

The Ultimate Goal
Total Customer Satisfaction

THE "TOTAL QUALITY" REVOLUTION

All manufacturing companies are paying attention these days to the concept of customer satisfaction. They are finally coming to recognize that it's a highly competitive world and that if you can't satisfy customers you may soon be out of business. References to "total quality," "continuous improvement," "excellence," and other quality-related concepts can be heard in virtually every manufacturing plant.

Three-Letter Programs

Today manufacturing companies of all sizes are trying, sometimes desperately, to improve the quality of their products and processes in order to stay ahead—or, in some cases, just to stay alive. This quality revolution has spawned a host of quality-related programs with three-letter names, from SPC (statistical process control) to JIT (just-in-time inventory). The big brother of all three-letter programs is TQM (total quality management), which has been embraced as the key to customer satisfaction by manufacturing firms around the country.

Even small manufacturers have jumped on the bandwagon. They are buying books and packing seminars on quality management, and are diligently filling in SPC charts in their plants. Most companies are afraid that their customers will not continue to buy their products unless they improve their product quality and their manufacturing process.

WHY "QUALITY" COMPANIES FAIL

I don't want to diminish the important contribution of the quality movement to the manufacturing sector of the US economy. This revolution in
quality is long overdue, and manufacturing companies have made great
strides in improving product and process quality in their plants as a result
of the movement.

Even though a great deal of attention is being paid to quality, many
companies are dying and many more are still losing customers. In *Marketing High Technology,* William Davidow pinpoints the real reason why:
"There are always lots of reasons why companies and industries die. . . .
But from the customer's point of view the reason is always the same.
Companies fail because they are incapable of delivering total customer
satisfaction."[1] Davidow's comment suggests that there may be a lot more
to "total customer satisfaction" than just product quality.

The Eight-Letter Word

What sometimes gets lost in all the three-letter programs is the eight-letter
word "customer." Ironically, the very people who triggered the quality
program in the first place are not always the focus of the program, because they are not easy to monitor or understand.

Most quality programs focus far more time and money on continuous
improvement of the internal production processes than on the monitoring
of customer needs and market changes. One reason for this is that,
whereas internal processes are easy to monitor and measure, customers
are difficult to monitor. They can be fickle, are often irrational, change
their minds frequently, and make excessive demands. No wonder manufacturers focus on products instead.

But never forget: customers are the folks who issue the purchase orders
that keep the plant doors open. No matter how difficult they are, unless
you monitor and satisfy them, your company may fail even if it produces
high-quality products.

Service Quality: The Missing Link

Another reason that small and midsize manufacturers lose customers despite their focus on "quality" is that they neglect the service dimension of
quality. Business customers don't just want high-quality products; they

want high-quality *solutions*. Solutions include customer services and support—not just products.

A machine can be manufactured and tested under the most rigorous quality standards and may even be accepted during the factory test as a "high-quality" product. But after installation at the customer's plant, the machine must be operated, maintained, updated, repaired, and serviced if it is going to *remain* a high-quality product. If for any reason a machine fails to maintain operational efficiency, the customer is going to be dissatisfied with the purchase, no matter how great the product looked when it was shipped out from your factory.

Figure 11–1 presents a checklist of some of the things that a manufacturer should be doing if it truly wants to satisfy customers. The checklist is not all-inclusive, but it is designed to help you answer a fundamental question: Is my company offering the level and quality of support and services necessary to achieve total customer satisfaction? If you can think of additional support services you can offer to customers, all the better.

Intangible Factors

There are other, intangible factors that go into achieving total customer satisfaction. These are not as easily measured as the services in Figure 11–1, but they are just as important, because they affect the customer's general perception of your products, your services, and your company.

Reliability. Customers judge the quality of a company not just on the basis of product reliability but on the company's ability to perform services dependably and in a timely matter.

Responsiveness. Customers judge quality partly on the basis of how willing and able the company is to help them use its products and resolve problems.

Assurance. This factor has to do with your ability to inspire trust and confidence in the customer, as a result of the actions, knowledge, and performance of your employees.

Empathy. Customers want you to stand in their shoes, to see problems from their point of view. This requires individualized attention to their problems and occasional visits to their plants.

These intangible factors contribute to the nebulous concept called *total customer satisfaction*. They dramatically affect the customer's perception

FIGURE 11–1

Customer Services Checklist (*What Does It Take to Satisfy Customers?*)

_____ 1. *Customer attitude.* Your first priority is to get customers back into service, and you always accept their word and assume they have a problem.

_____ 2. *Tailor the strategy.* You have developed specific services that support and fit customer groups.

_____ 3. *Quotations.* Your sales staff can offer customers complete information with short turnaround times.

_____ 4. *Manuals and documentation.* Your manuals are written in simple language and in a how-to format, and are tailored to the needs of specific customer groups.

_____ 5. *Customer hotline.* Your customers can reach you after hours and at your expense.

_____ 6. *Knowledgeable technical sales support.* You make sure that your technical support people have all the tools and knowledge needed to solve customer problems.

_____ 7. *Factory tests.* You ensure that part of your overall product quality program is making sure all factory demonstrations have excellent results.

_____ 8. *Employee training.* You have an ongoing program of product and service training. You consider the training time an investment, and you consider training to be as important as selling.

_____ 9. *Customer service training.* You invest in factory customer training as well as traveling seminars to ensure that your customers will be able to troubleshoot, maintain, and operate your products on their own.

_____ 10. *24-hour parts service.* You have developed a rescue program that can respond to customer emergencies.

_____ 11. *Program updates.* You make product improvements and updates a customer satisfaction tool and part of your value-added product/service package.

_____ 12. *Packaging.* You spend the time to make the packaging of your products a pleasant surprise.

_____ 13. *Product quality.* You assume that the best customer support is a good-quality product the first time, and you let the customer's audit drive your program.

of the quality of your company. Remember, you should base your quality improvement efforts on the *customer's* perception, not your own.

Perhaps perceptions are "only" the psychological side of customer services, but this does not diminish their importance. Whether a customer decides to buy from a competitor because your product doesn't work or because a service rep failed to return a call promptly makes no difference. Either way, you've lost the order. In the final analysis, total customer satisfaction is about customers' perceptions of your product quality and your services, your company, and the use of your product over time.

A MOVING TARGET

We have defined the elusive concept called *total customer satisfaction* as including product quality, customer services and support, and customer perceptions. Yet another factor must be added into the equation—change.

Customers and markets are dynamic. A product that was considered high-quality last year may not solve the customer's problems this year. Service that was considered excellent last year may be the minimum requirement now. The competition may offer more value-added services to the customer and put your company at a service disadvantage. Your relationship with the customer may change because of their changing perceptions of intangible and tangible factors.

Any quality or customer satisfaction program must take into consideration that customer requirements are going to change continuously. If you want to achieve and maintain total customer satisfaction, you must constantly refine your products and services in response to the changing needs of your customers.

How can you set up an efficient system for achieving total customer satisfaction when customers constantly change their requirements? The large-corporation solution to monitoring customer needs is another three-letter manufacturing program called *quality function deployment,* (QFD) and also referred to as *the house of quality.* QFD is an honest effort to translate customer needs into information that can be used by every department of the organization. It consists of a complex, nine-stage process that involves the development of an elaborate planning matrix.

If you have the staff, the budget, and the time, QFD may be the ultimate process for monitoring customer needs. There's no room to discuss the details here, but they can be found in numerous quality books. However, I know of few SMMs that have the resources or patience to mount a QFD program.

Fortunately, there are many practical, effective ways of monitoring customer needs that don't require large staffs or sophisticated methods. Following are eight simple suggestions for continuously monitoring your customers' needs and measuring customer satisfaction, based on the information presented in this book.

EIGHT SIMPLE WAYS TO MONITOR CUSTOMER SATISFACTION

1. *Customer satisfaction surveys.* Make a commitment to starting an ongoing survey to find out how satisfied your customers are with your products and services. (See Figures 2–5 and 2–6 for sample surveys.)

2. *Most valuable customers.* Select a few MVCs and make sure that your products and services are meeting their needs. (See Figure 2–3, "The Acid Test.")

3. *Lost order analysis.* Find out which customers and prospects are buying competitor's products, and why. (See "Lost Order Analysis" in Chapter 2).

4. *Competitor comparisons.* Make a list of the most critical product and service factors, and find out how customers compare your company to competitors on these factors. (See Figure 4–2, "Ask a Customer.")

5. *New products .* Describe the customer needs that products under development will satisfy. (See Figure 6–5, "Screening Matrix"; Figure 6–6, "User Benefit Checklist"; and Step 9: Develop the Product/Service Package in Chapter 6.)

6. *Customer satisfaction log.* Maintain a log of all product, warranty, customer service, and other customer satisfaction problems, and evaluate current service. (See Figure 11–1, Customer Services Checklist.)

7. *Field reports.* Develop a system of sales and service field reports to monitor customer complaints and problems.

8. *Satisfaction committee.* Create a management committee whose function is to review all customer satisfaction problems and to take swift action to correct them.

A HOLISTIC APPROACH

Achievement of total customer satisfaction requires taking a holistic approach to serving customers—an approach that includes improving product quality and customer services, awareness of customer perceptions, and monitoring of customer needs. At the heart of this approach is listening to customers all the time and allowing them to drive your business—which is a fundamental principle of business marketing. When SMMs say their goal is high quality and total customer satisfaction, they are in essence saying they want to be customer and market driven. In the final analysis, business marketing can be defined as a total business philosophy whose goal is achieving total customer satisfaction. This requires moving from an operations or product-oriented point of view to a market orientation. This is not an easy journey for most manufacturers, as Charles Ames predicted.

In 1970, Ames published an article in *Harvard Business Review*. This article has become a classic. In it, Ames stressed the importance of adopting a market orientation and anticipated the difficulties manufacturers would face in making the shift. He predicted that manufacturing companies everywhere were going to be faced with more competition and a more challenging business environment. Unless they developed an external (customer) focus, he wrote, they would begin losing in the markets they had once dominated. He also predicted that it would be a hard task to convert an "operations-oriented company to one that is market-oriented."[2]

Ames was correct on all counts. American manufacturers have had a tough time adapting to an external focus and becoming market-oriented, customer-driven companies. In light of the decline and failure of many of the biggest US flagship companies in recent years, his statements were prophetic, to say the least.

Coming Full Circle

Market-oriented and *customer-driven* are old concepts whose time has apparently come, now that the very survival of many US firms is threatened. Manufacturers are finally accepting the idea that becoming market-oriented and customer-driven is essential for their survival and success. It has taken US manufacturing firms an enormous amount of time and discovery to accept what Charles Ames and other savvy marketers knew decades ago. As T. S. Eliot wrote:

> We shall not cease from exploration
> And the end of all our exploring
> Will be to arrive where we started
> And know the place for the very first time.[2]

NOTES

1. William Davidow, *Marketing High Technology* (New York: The Free Press, A Division of McMillan, Inc., 1986), p. 172.

2. Copyright © 1990 by the president and fellows of Harvard College; all rights reserved. Reprinted by permission of *Harvard Business Review.* "Trappings vs. Substance in Industrial Marketing," by Charles Ames, July–August 1990, p. 102.

3. T S Eliot, "Little Gidding," *Scrutiny* XI, no. 3 (Spring 1943), pp. 216–19. First published in America in "The Importance of Scrutiny" by Eric Bentley (George W. Stewart, Inc., 1948; New York: Grove Press, 1957).

Index